POPULAR OBJECTIONS

TO

UNITARIAN CHRISTIANITY

CONSIDERED AND ANSWERED.

IN SEVEN DISCOURSES.

By GEORGE W. BURNAP,
PASTOR OF THE FIRST INDEPENDENT CHURCH OF BALTIMORE.

"In meekness instructing those that oppose themselves."
PAUL.

FIFTH EDITION.

BOSTON:
CROSBY, NICHOLS, AND COMPANY,
111 WASHINGTON STREET.
1855.

CAMBRIDGE:
METCALF AND COMPANY,
PRINTERS TO THE UNIVERSITY.

PREFACE.

THE following Discourses were delivered in the First Independent Church of Baltimore, immediately after its re-opening, having undergone extensive repairs. The author took the opportunity presented by the concourse of strangers which resorted to the church during some of the succeeding Sundays, to answer some of the leading objections which are everywhere current against the faith which is there inculcated. He conceives that there is much need of such publications.

Since the first promulgation of Christianity, nothing has been more misapprehended and misrepresented than Unitarianism at the present day. It is not allowed to make its defence. It cannot obtain a hearing. It is classified with every thing that is bad, and then people are warned against looking into it, or even hearing an exposition of its doctrines.

Unitarians are accused on all occasions of being unbelievers, — of setting reason above Scripture, — of expecting to be saved by their own merits, — of denying the Atonement, — of mutilating and explaining away the Scriptures, — of being merely moral men, and preaching mere morality, — of not being Evangelical Christians, — of advocating a system which tends to infidelity, &c.

It was the object of these Discourses, to meet and answer these objections. After their delivery, it was suggested to the author that they would be useful when published in the form of a book. It is with the hope that they may do good, in removing prejudice and in enlightening the minds of the inquiring, that they are now given to the public.

In the concluding Discourse, on the Unitarianism of Doctor Watts, there will be found some interesting facts relating to the religious opinions and theological inquiries of that eminent Christian and devout Psalmist. It will be objected by some, perhaps, that the extracts are *ex parte*, and taken out of their connection. It may be answered, that the space of a single discourse did not permit the subject to be treated in any other way. I merely ask the reader to consider with himself whether such paragraphs could have been written by a Trinitarian in any connection. The extracts are made from the London edition of the year 1810.

CONTENTS.

DISCOURSE I.

The Position of Unitarianism defined.

DISCOURSE II.

Unitarians not Infidels.

DISCOURSE III

Explaining the Bible and explaining it away.

DISCOURSE IV.

Unitarianism not mere Morality.

DISCOURSE V.

Unitarianism Evangelical Christianity.

DISCOURSE VI.

Unitarianism does not tend to Unbelief.

DISCOURSE VII.

Doctor Watts a Unitarian.

DISCOURSE I.

THE POSITION OF UNITARIANISM DEFINED.

JESUS SAITH UNTO HER, WOMAN, BELIEVE ME, THE HOUR COMETH WHEN YE SHALL NEITHER IN THIS MOUNTAIN, NOR YET AT JERUSALEM, WORSHIP THE FATHER. YE WORSHIP YE KNOW NOT WHAT. WE KNOW WHAT WE WORSHIP; FOR SALVATION IS OF THE JEWS. BUT THE HOUR COMETH, AND NOW IS, WHEN THE TRUE WORSHIPPERS SHALL WORSHIP THE FATHER IN SPIRIT AND IN TRUTH; FOR THE FATHER SEEKETH SUCH TO WORSHIP HIM. GOD IS A SPIRIT; AND THEY THAT WORSHIP HIM MUST WORSHIP HIM IN SPIRIT AND IN TRUTH. — John iv. 21 - 24.

THESE are some of the sublimest words which were ever uttered on earth. It is in partial fulfilment of them that we, at the distance of more than eighteen centuries, "with half the convex globe between," are assembled to worship God in the name of Christ in this beautiful temple built upon this distant shore, when the temple of Jerusalem, which then glittered afar in Oriental splendor, has long ago been razed to its foundations. I shall not attempt to describe the joy with which we again assemble in this sacred place. To many of you it has become endeared by the most tender and holy associations;

with the Sabbath's rest and the Sabbath's musings, with the soul's most consecrated hours of communion with God, with the divine teachings of Christ's blessed Gospel, with the moving symbols of his sorrows and his death, with the anthems of God's praise, with the hopes and anticipations of heaven, with the memory of kindred and companions, who, you trust, are now worshipping in that temple not made with hands eternal in the heavens.

I have thought to add interest to this first day of our restoration to our renovated house of prayer, by rehearsing the history of this church and religious society, by re-stating the principles upon which it was founded, the objects to which its energies are directed, the changes which have passed over the religious world since its establishment, and the prospects which the future presents of the dissemination of those great truths which it maintains as vital to Christianity and to man.

On the 12th of October, 1816, there appeared in one or more of the Baltimore newspapers the following advertisement: — "Divine service will be performed by the Rev. Doctor Freeman of Boston to-morrow at the Hall belonging to Mr. Gibney in South Charles Street, to commence at 11 o'clock A. M. and at half past 3 P. M."

Accordingly, at the appointed hours, an audience assembled and services were held. On the next Sunday, public worship was again celebrated at the same hours and in the same place. Those who listened to the exercises of those two days had been accustomed to worship in the various churches in the city ; but they now heard an exposition of the doctrines of Christianity, as it seemed to them, more reasonable, consistent, and edifying, than any to which they had ever given their attention.

To many, perhaps most, of the hearers, the denomination to which the speaker belonged was wholly unknown. Their judgment of what he uttered was formed, therefore, either without prejudice, or in opposition to the bias there always exists against any thing that is new. A simultaneous desire sprang up in the minds of many who were there, to procure foı themselves and their children a stated ministry by which such views of Christianity might be inculcated and maintained.

But who was Doctor Freeman, and why does he preach in a hall ? Among all the various denominations of Christians, is there no pulpit in the city to which he may be invited ? Not one. He had been almost isolated for more than thirty years for conscience' sake. For more than thirty years, in the way called heresy he and the people of his charge had worshipped the God of their fathers. His personal history is, that he was a graduate of Harvard University of the class of 1777.

He pursued his preparatory theological studies principally at Cambridge, and in October, 1782, became Reader at "King's Chapel," an Episcopal church in Boston, and in the April following was chosen Pastor of the church. He continued to read the Episcopal Book of Common Prayer till 1785, when a committee of the proprietors was appointed to revise that manual of devotion, and present it in a form more agreeable, as they thought, to the word of God. The result of their labor was the production, in substance, of the "Chapel Liturgy," a beautiful and almost faultless form of public devotions, now used by that ancient society. This change, and as they thought reform, was brought about mainly by the studies and ministrations of their pastor, who gave a course of lectures explanatory of the Scriptures in relation to those doctrines which were left out of their new book of prayer. Thus the most ancient Episcopal church in New England became the first Unitarian church in America.

Nothing, then, could have been more appropriate, than that the patriarch of Unitarianism in America should have been the founder of Unitarianism in Maryland.

The desire to have a church in Baltimore, modelled upon the simple principles of the Gospel, excited by the preaching of Doctor Freeman, found expression in a meeting held by several of the citizens on the 10th day of February, 1817, for the purpose of organizing a religious society, and taking into consideration the best means of erecting a building for public worship.

At this meeting they adopted a constitution, and gave to the society the legal title of "The First Independent Church of Baltimore." They also appointed nine trustees to superintend the concerns of the society and the erection of the building. The corner-stone was laid on the 5th day of June, 1817, in the presence of all the trustees, most of the subscribers, and many others.

In the centre of the stone, a plate was deposited, bearing the following inscription : —

In Greek, — "To the King eternal, immortal, invisible, the only wise God."

In English, – "This corner-stone of the First Independent Church of Baltimore was laid on the 5th day of June, 1817, under the direction of the following Trustees and Building Committee, viz. Henry Payson, Ezekiel Freeman, Cumberland D. Williams, James W. McCulloh, Tobias Watkins, Nathaniel Williams, William Child, Charles H. Appleton, John H. Poor, and Isaac Phillips. Maximilian Godfroy, Architect, and John Ready, Builder."

The church was completed in October, 1818, and dedicated on the 29th of the same month by Dr. Freeman, and the Rev. Mr. Colman, of Hingham, Mass., Dr. Freeman preaching the sermon.

The pulpit was supplied by different preachers from Boston and the neighbourhood, till May, 1819, when the Rev. Jared Sparks was ordained as the first pastor of this church ; his ordination took place on the 5th of the month, and Mr., afterwards Dr. Channing, of Boston, delivered the customary discourse.

The 5th of May, 1819, was a memorable day in the theological history of this country. It might be called the Pentecost of American Unitarianism. In setting apart a minister to teach a faith, which, although the most ancient, appeared to the community in which it was to be preached comparatively a new doctrine, Mr. Channing thought it incumbent on him to make an open, plain, and candid statement of the principles which this new edifice was raised to maintain and disseminate. Into better hands that task could not have fallen. Circumstances made that discourse a confession of faith, a manifesto of principles, a declaration of independence, to a new association of the followers of Christ. For its purpose it was perfect. So clear are its statements, so simple its language, so grand and comprehensive the truths it unfolds, such earnestness, conviction, and candor pervade it all, that it leaves very little to be desired, and very little to be added. It made a profound impression. None who heard it will ever forget that day. Its publication, which took place immediately after, was followed by still more important results. On the printed page it appeared no less striking, original, powerful, and convincing, than it had done in delivery. It spread over the country with wonderful rapidity. It was reprinted and circulated by thousands, and no pamphlet, with one exception, and that a political publication, ever attracted in this country so wide and universal attention.

Its author, before not widely, though favorably, known, soon rose to the highest literary eminence, and has been since acknowledged as one of the greatest masters of the English tongue, even in the jealous judgment of our mother land. His works are more read in England than those of any other theologian. Almost every year produces a new edition of them in this country, and this sermon, incorporated into his works, has, on the whole, been more read than any other, perhaps, that has been delivered in modern times.

This visit of Mr. Channing to Baltimore was the cause of a religious movement in another city, quite as important as this. On his way home, he stopped a short time at New York. His friends attempted to procure him a place to preach in, on Sunday. To obtain a church for him was hopeless, and he held services in a private house. Those services gave being to a religious society, which has since expanded into two of the most beautiful and well-attended churches in the city.

But to return to Baltimore. The plain avowal of principles and candid declaration of purposes made by Mr. Channing, while they gave clearness of view, definiteness of doctrine, and concentration of action to the new church, drew more sharply the line of demarcation by which it was separated from the rest of the Christian world, and perhaps made it more difficult to obtain even a hearing for a theology so divergent from the doctrines inculcated in most of the pulpits in the city. The whole population was moved. Clergy and people vied with each other in heaping opprobrium upon the new sect. The churches rang from Sabbath to Sabbath with warning and denunciation. The whole vocabulary of abuse was ransacked and exhausted for terms of reprobation and contempt sufficiently strong to express the general feelings of abhorrence and detestation towards this association of the disciples of Christ. Not only was their faith assailed as dangerous and damnable, but their personal characters were aspersed as immoral and unworthy of the esteem of their fellow-citizens.

And what had they done to deserve all this? They had withdrawn from other churches to establish a worship, as they honestly believed, more consonant with the truth of God's word. They were doing what they conscientiously thought to be their duty. They were exercising a right guaranteed to every citizen in this country, of worshipping God according to the dictates of his own conscience. Their very position was a sufficient pledge of their sincerity. It was no pleasure, and certainly no profit, to them to dissent from their fellow-Christians. They would have better consulted their own peace by remaining where they were, and silently acquiescing in modes of worship which their judgments could not approve. They did not establish this church in the wantonness of self-will, or that they might from it hurl anathema and defiance upon the whole Christian world. They denied no man's Christianity on account of the errors of faith which they apprehended him to entertain. They condemned no man for his creed; they simply stated what seemed to them true, and what false, in it, according to the light of the sacred Scriptures. They saw and acknowledged what appeared to them to be good and true in every system of faith and discipline which prevailed around them.

In the Catholics, they recognized the most ancient embodiment of the Christian faith and ritual. Some of the brightest ornaments of the Christian name have been of its communion. In its spirit and its worship, they recognized the manifestation of the profoundest reverence that has ever been exhibited in the world, but, in their judgment, a reverence unreasoning and indiscriminate, which has gathered around the accidents of Christianity with quite as much devotion as around its real substance; a reverence which embraces, with equal intensity, the accretions which a thousand years of intellectual darkness through which it passed have associated with its essential rites and doctrines, as the great truths which its ritual is intended to represent and perpetuate.

On entering a Catholic church, they saw an image

of the crucified Saviour, before which the multitude bowed down. Their hearts, too, were moved by the sculptured agonies of the man of sorrows, and it was no want of affectionate reverence which led them to question the propriety of such an exhibition. But they could not avoid recollecting the prohibition, dating fifteen centuries earlier than Christianity itself, — "Thou shalt not make unto thee any graven image, or the likeness of any thing that is in heaven above or the earth beneath. Thou shalt not bow down thyself to them nor serve them." This prohibition is peremptory, positive, and absolute, and made by Him who created the human heart, and who knows infinitely better than we the perversions to which the religious principle is liable.

And even if images were permitted in Christian churches, they felt that, by the selection of the saddest scene of Christ's history as the only one presented to the senses, the Catholic Church had given an undue shade of gloom to his whole religion. The cross of Christ was thus made to cast its dark shadow, not only over the whole life of Christ, but over the whole life of the Christian world, and caused it, in the apprehension of multitudes, to be constituted of penances and mortifications, rather than cheerful and grateful obedience. The darkness that settled on the hills of Judea at the hour of the crucifixion did not last long. The bright sun shone before and after. There was an hour when Christ rejoiced, and the mount of transfiguration must be a better representation of the glory and joy to which he ascended, than the cross of Calvary which he left behind. The altar service seemed to them rather Judaic than Christian, inasmuch as the main employment and office of Christ was that of Teacher. He proclaimed himself "the Light of the world," and his parting charge to his Apostles was, "Go, teach all nations."

Altars were done away. Sacrifices for ever ceased with the abolition of the Jewish religion, of which they made a part.

The celebration of public worship in a dead language — a language which has ceased to be spoken for a thousand years — seemed to them to savour of an unquestioning attachment to arbitrary and obsolete forms, rather than of a wise and allowable conformity to the altered condition of the world; and the invocation of the Virgin, a mortal like ourselves, made it impossible for them to acquiesce in the ritual of the Catholic Church.

In the Methodists, the next most numerous denomination by which they were surrounded, they recognized a living and vital member of Christ's body. In their genial, social, and earnest spirit, they saw a resemblance to primitive Christianity, when "the disciples were of one accord in one place," "and did eat their meat with gladness and singleness of heart."

They looked on Wesley as an instrument in the

hands of Providence of breaking the paralyzing spell of a ritual religion, and adapting the administration of the Gospel to the poor, the ignorant, and the isolated. They saw, in some parts of their church organization, and in their freedom from written creeds, an approach to that liberty wherewith Christ has made his disciples free.

Yet there was one feature of their worship which rendered it impossible for the founders of this church to join habitually in it. No small part of their devotions was directed to Christ. God is the only proper object of religious worship. He has strictly forbidden divine homage to be addressed to any other being besides himself. And Christ, before he left the world, was equally explicit in enjoining it on his disciples, not to pray to him, when he should be exalted to heaven, but to pray to God in his name. "And in that day ye shall ask me nothing. Verily, verily, I say unto you, whatsoever ye shall ask the Father in my name, he will give it you."

To those who built this house as the place of their worship, the Presbyterian door to the fold of Christ was closed, for over it was written a creed which it was impossible for them to subscribe, and which said, in effect, — "Let no one enter here who does not admit the tri-personality of God, the total, constitutional corruption of human nature, and the exclusive agency of God in every act of man that is acceptable in his sight." It was impossible for them to approach the table of communion in that church, for it was fenced about with execrations on those who should partake of the elements, not believing that their humble Master, who died on the cross to save them, was at the same time the ever-living Jehovah, to whom he commended his departing spirit, and to whom he prayed, "My God, my God, why hast thou forsaken me?"

Many had found refuge in the Episcopal Church. Its more rational teaching and milder discipline they thought more calculated to embrace and edify the various shades of belief which will ever be found among imperfect and fallible mortals. To them there was an intrinsic respectability in its dignified forms, and a conservatism in its stability, which contrasted well with the more informal modes of organization and worship. In the religion of the Prayer Book they could acquiesce, for to it had been contributed the piety of many ages. Some of its devotions, for tenderness and sublimity, are nowhere exceeded out of the Psalms of the ancient people of God. But its theology they conceived to be unfounded in the Scriptures, and irreconcilable to right reason when calmly examined by an enlightened and reflecting mind. Its articles of faith were adopted in England in the twilight of the Reformation, as a matter of state policy, and were a compromise between the advancing Protestantism of the school of Geneva and the receding dogmas of the Papal ages. Their only pretence to authority at the present day, and in this country, is their being contained in the same binding with some of the most exquisite devotions in the English tongue. Not more than half of those, perhaps, who use the devotions ever read the articles of faith.

Had the creed and the devotions been kept separate, the Prayer Book would have been nearly unexceptionable. But the most unscriptural, and, in their judgment, objectionable, part of the creed was woven into the liturgy, so as to implicate those who joined in it in a breach of the first commandment. The God who gave the first commandment must be supposed to be the same who gave the fourth. In the fourth he is identified as "Jehovah, who made heaven and earth and sea, and all that in them is." That Being, in the first commandment, enjoins, — "Thou shalt have no other gods before me." But he who joins in the Episcopal service first prays, as he ought, to "God, the Father of heaven." Then he prays to another God, — "O God, the Son." Not only is he another God, but he has another name and another function, — "O God, the Son, Redeemer of the world." God is a spirit, but this second God has a body, and is addressed as having human attributes, parts, and passions, and having been subjected to human sufferings: — "By thy holy nativity and circumcision, by thine agony and bloody sweat."

A God who has been born and circumcised must be another God, essentially as well as numerically different from the Almighty Creator of heaven and earth, who inhabiteth immensity and eternity, whom no eye hath seen or can see, the blessed and only Potentate.

Now there is no such God as God the Son, there is no such name, there are no such words as "God the Son" in the Scriptures.

Then a third God is introduced, with still another name and function, — "O God, the Holy Ghost, proceeding from the Father and the Son." There is no such God as "God the Holy Ghost" revealed to us in the Scriptures. There is not a single instance of worship addressed to the Holy Ghost, from the beginning of the Bible to the end. There is no such name or phrase as "God the Holy Ghost" in the sacred writings.

The believers in "one God and one mediator between God and men, the man Christ Jesus," could not but feel aggrieved that such unscriptural expressions should have been incorporated into the forms of public worship. Their devotions were disturbed, their edification obstructed, and they therefore sought a place where they could worship God in the name of Christ, instead of worshipping Christ as "God the Son."

Another reason for dissent from the Episcopal service was the repetition of a creed of human device This appeared to them especially objectionable in a Protestant sect, as the only authority upon which the creeds are received is that of the Church of Rome whose general authority that sect had rejected, and whose infallibility it had denied. From that Church it had consented to take a creed, or rather two creeds, in England three creeds, all inconsistent with each other, and by constant public repetition to hand them down unexamined and unchanged from age to age.

For these causes, the founders of this church withdrew from the various communions with which they had been associated, and sought for themselves a new place of worship. And they were true to their principles. They deposited in this desk a copy of the sacred Scriptures, as the only foundation of their faith, the only infallible depository of truth, the only sure guide of life. They opened the font of baptism to all who felt it their duty to consecrate their children to God, to Christ, and the Holy Spirit. They spread the table of communion to all who acknowledged their allegiance to Christ as "the Way, the Truth, and the Life." They repelled no humble disciple from it by unintelligible mysteries or incomprehensible articles of faith. They published no creed. They left every man to form his own. They did better than to publish a creed. They made a selection from the sacred Scriptures of the most striking texts which embodied their faith, inculcated their obligations, and expressed their hopes and aspirations, and wrote them down on those beautiful tablets to be seen and read of all men, as a public declaration of their standing as believers in God, and in the divine mediation of Christ, and as a perpetual and emphatic, though silent, refutation of the slanders everywhere propagated against them as atheists and infidels.

In their first clergyman they had selected a man abundantly able to make good their position, and to vindicate to the world the faith which they professed. The next year after his ordination, he published a volume of "Letters on the Ministry, Ritual, and Doctrines of the Protestant Episcopal Church," which placed him at once in the first rank of theological scholars in this country. This was followed up, in 1821, by the establishment of a religious periodical, "The Unitarian Miscellany," a work published monthly, and filled with thorough and able discussions of the theological topics of the day, but chiefly devoted to the statement and defence of the doctrines of Christianity as understood by Unitarians. The matter for this periodical was mainly furnished by Mr. Sparks, in addition to the labor of writing for his weekly ministrations. This was kept up for nearly three years. In this double office of preacher and editor, an amount of intellectual toil was sustained by him truly astonishing, and credible only to those who have measured the capacities of human endurance, and learned the grand secret of the economy of time.

It would be difficult to find, in the whole range of

theological literature, three volumes of equal compass, which contain so much and such accurate information on the most interesting subjects of religious inquiry. It is rare to find in theological controversy so much candor of statement, and such fairness of reasoning, such firmness of persuasion, united with so much charity for the opinions of others. They are a monument of theological attainment and literary industry, which sets a high mark for the clergy of our country.

But their author had undertaken labors too great for the time as well as the strength of one man, and his health at length sunk under them, and he retired from the ministry to win a wider fame and a still higher reputation among the historians of his country.

His place as pastor of the church and editor of the Miscellany was temporarily supplied by the Rev. Mr., afterwards Dr. Greenwood, who had lately retired in ill health from Church Green in Boston, and had sought restoration in a milder climate. Under his management the Miscellany lost nothing of its literary power, though perhaps something of the depth of its theological discussions. As a preacher, Mr. Greenwood had few superiors. He was made for a clergyman. His taste in composition was perfect, his voice deep and sonorous, his manner serious, affectionate, and impressive. And he was long a bright and shining light in the churches. On the restoration of his health, he returned to Boston, and became the colleague of Dr. Freeman, whose history has already been narrated. With his departure, the Miscellany was discontinued, having reached its sixth volume, and done much good. Its circulation was extensive, and it had enlightened many dark minds, removed many prejudices, and convinced many inquirers that religion was consistent with reason, and Christianity unencumbered with irreconcilable contradictions.

From 1824 to 1827, the pulpit was supplied by different clergymen, generally from Boston and the neighbourhood, many of them highly distinguished by position, talents, and acquirements. In September of 1827, the present pastor preached for the first time from this pulpit. In the following April he was ordained, and from that time to this the pulpit has never been supplied by the society for a single Sabbath. In the space of fifteen years, the church has been closed but three half-days on account of the pastor's failure to officiate.

Since the very beginning, no religious society ever struggled with more difficulties, or surmounted them with more indomitable courage and perseverance. It has been twice nearly prostrated by commercial revulsions, and has often suffered severe losses by emigration. However, "having obtained help of God, we continue unto this day." The smiles of a gracious Providence have been granted to the members of this society in their temporal affairs in more than ordinary measure, and this beautiful and renovated temple is witness that they are willing to set apart a portion of God's blessings to beautify his sanctuary and to honor his worship. "Pray for the peace of Jerusalem. They shall prosper that love thee."

But the building of this church was not an isolated nor an inconsequential event. It was an epoch in the theological history of the country. Its effects were immediate and decisive, and their operation has gone on deepening and widening from that day to this. The sentiments which were here openly professed had been silently spreading in various parts of the country for more than a quarter of a century. In New England especially, many independent inquirers had, without consultation or concert, arrived at nearly the same conclusions from a careful examination of the sacred Scriptures. But their opinions, when known, did not exclude them from ministerial intercourse with their brethren in the same communion. The publication of the discourse of Mr. Channing at the ordination of Mr. Sparks revealed to each party the ground on which they stood. It was attacked by the theological professors at Andover, and defended by those at Cambridge ; the whole community became interested, and took part with one side or the other of the disputants. The Orthodox withdrew from ministerial intercourse with those who approved the theological doctrines of that discourse, and thus the Unitarians, as they were called, were forced to assume the position of a distinct religious denomination. From that day to this, they have acted as such. They have had their own theological schools, their own periodicals, their own conventions. They have been continually growing in numbers, strength, zeal, and enterprise.

This separation, by the Unitarians unsought and unpremeditated, has led to some most important results; one of which has been the development of an original, independent, theological literature, drawn from individual study of the sacred Scriptures and all the phenomena of humanity and religious experience, wholly unbiased by previously existing creeds and systems of divinity. The list of Unitarian books produced within thirty years would furnish a large theological library, — as large as a person of ordinary leisure would read in a lifetime. These works are not doctrinal alone. Many of them are practical and devotional, and minister not only light to the understanding, but warmth to the heart. Inculcating a faith which is consistent with reason, instead of contradictory to it, they make religion a subject of interest to all. Starting from the point, that the object of Christianity is to change, modify, or develop the human character, not to alter the human constitution, they propose an object which is within the scope of human endeavours, and not placed without the compass of human capacities.

If Unitarianism as a denomination had done nothing else than produce this powerful and diversified theological literature, it would have abundantly justified its existence to the world. It is books which form the opinions and the churches of coming ages. The dogmas of this age are the fruits of the thinking, the writing, the books, of the ages that are gone, and the only possible way in which the future ages can be made to differ from the past is by substituting other books to be the manuals of their education and the guides of their inquiries.

During the thirty years of our denominational existence, great changes have been passing over the whole religious world. Even Catholicism, which is the type and representative of conservatism, has been moved to its centre. Every denomination throughout Christendom has been divided into two parties, one advocating progress, the other rest. Most especially is this the case in this country, where the press is free and prolific beyond all former example. Not only have parties been formed, but communions have been divided, immense ecclesiastical organizations have been sundered, and the points of difference have often been the same which have made us a distinct denomination.

It would be arrogance in us to attribute to our theological labors any considerable part of this great change. It is enough for us to have the confidence that we have contributed something towards it.

That those great and extensive movements are in the same direction with our own is at least demonstration that our movement is in coincidence with the tendencies of the age.

There are hundreds and thousands in all communions who sympathize with us, who conscientiously believe that we have arrived nearer than any other sect at the truth of the Gospel.

I have been often led to doubt whether there are, at the present day, any real Trinitarians. The test of this is their own private devotions. Christians in public will fall in without question with established forms, and apparently acquiesce in phraseology with which they are by no means satisfied. But in private their real belief comes out. I question whether one person in a thousand of nominal Trinitarians ever prays in private to the Holy Ghost. And he who does not pray to the Holy Ghost is practically not a Trinitarian. The Lord's prayer, the model of all devotion, passes over the doctrine of the Trinity in the profoundest silence.

There are clergymen not a few, who have investigated for themselves till they have found that their own views, when defined to their own minds, are nearer to the personal unity of God than to the old Trinitarian system. But in their present position, the less inquiry the more peace, because their own minds are not free. The conclusions of their inquiries are forestalled by their previous ecclesiastical connections and engagements. They have subscribed a creed, or they belong to an organization which requires and enforces one, and therefore their lips are sealed.

And here I should fail to do justice to the wisdom, courage, and fidelity of the founders of this church, if I omitted to mention a vital principle which they incorporated into the constitution of their religious association, and made prominent in its very name, that of congregational independence. They had clearly seen that this principle is an indispensable condition to the enjoyment of that religious liberty wherewith Christ has made us free. Subscription to a creed, the association of churches together on the basis of a creed, enforced upon all their members on pain of excommunication or disparagement of any kind, involves a surrender of all those principles on which the Protestants separated from the Catholics, and upon which they have maintained a theological controversy for three hundred years. If, with the Bible in my hands, and all the means of an independent examination now extant at my command, I allow another man to write my creed, and swear to teach his interpretation, however different it may be from that which my own investigation convinces me is the true one, I am false to my allegiance to the truth, an allegiance which I never can abjure. It is the same to me, as far as principle is concerned, whether I adopt the Westminster Confession, or the creed of the Council of Nice.

Had the creed-making power been permitted to rule unbroken, Protestantism never could have had an existence. Luther would have perished in his first protest. So, in this country, if the creed-making power had had its own way, Unitarianism could never have come into being. Had church and state been united, or had the Episcopal Church possessed a stringent organization, the founder of this church would not have been permitted to revise the Prayer Book according to the word of God.

And now and here, among most Protestant sects, there are nearly the same impediments to the investigation of truth, that there were in the Papal Church at the Reformation. The candid inquirer, the honest preacher, who happens to travel out of the circumference of a human formulary of faith, is immediately assailed, and compelled to pass through the same fiery ordeal which was endured by the first martyrs, with the exception that ecclesiastical laws do not now touch the life.

This beautiful temple, then, stands dedicated, not alone to the inculcation of religious truth, but to the establishment and maintenance of religious liberty, by which alone religious truth can be discovered and secured. That freedom is found alone in Congregational Independency, in which every man, clergyman, and layman has guaranteed to him, as his natural and indefeasible right, the liberty to interpret the Scriptures by the light which God has given him.

Its vast expense, its exquisite symmetry, were originally an emphatic testimony to the world of the priceless estimate which its founders placed upon what seemed to them a sound and a true theology. In the same spirit it is, that their successors have restored the waste of years, and set it in order afresh for the worship of God. By it they declare the deep conviction of their hearts, that a sound theology is the first of human wants. They see and feel, that men must and will have a religion. The Sabbath is set apart mainly to religious instruction. The mass of the people will be taught something. What shall it be? Shall it be a system of doctrines at war with reason, Scripture, and moral feeling? Or shall it be a system of doctrines consistent with them all?

To them it seems a sore evil, that the precious time devoted to sacred instruction should be worse than wasted in discussions of metaphysical divinity, wholly aside from the word of God, and the common and practical duties of every-day life. It seems to them a great public injury, that the mass of the people should be taught that the corruption which prevails among them is constitutional and inevitable, instead of being their own work in the abuse of the nature and faculties that God has given them. They see no hope for the moral regeneration of the world, so long as men are taught, that, in the condition in which God creates them, sin is their appropriate, their necessary, their only possible work; that not more than one person in a hundred has within him the elements which are necessary to moral probation. It seems to them, that by these dogmas all motive to the religious education of children is paralyzed. There is nothing religious in children to educate. They can do nothing, in consequence of their education, until Omnipotence sees fit to create them anew. Probation, in any equitable sense of the term, does not commence with rational existence, but in those who are elected, at that point of time when the constitutional deficiency of their nature is supplied by grace, and in the non-elect it never commences at all. Then the doctrine of atonement, a cardinal doctrine of the New Testament, as long as it is represented as an agency to reconcile God to man, instead of man to God, must, as far as it has any influence, nullify the moral efficiency of the practical doctrines of Christ. A theology which misrepresents God and man, and the relations which subsist between them, must be essentially wrong.

Yet, with these convictions, we are no sectarians. We do not compass sea and land to make a proselyte. We have no ambition to propagate a name, or to marshal hosts of mere partisans. Our only desire, before God, is to propagate the simple truth. We aspire to no other name than that of Christian. We consider it the hardest part of our lot, and the saddest fact in the condition of the world, that in the Christian Church we should derive a sectarian name from maintaining the fundamental truth both of Judaism and Christianity, the numerical and personal unity of God, — "Jehovah our God, Jehovah is one."

So thoroughly convinced are we of the truth of our principles, so deeply persuaded are we that they are the simple teachings of God's word, and that the time must come when they will be acknowledged by all candid inquirers, that it does not move us that the world goeth not out after us, that our census is no greater among Christian denominations. Nothing true and good has ever met from the world a tumultuous reception. Christianity itself began in an upper chamber, and the first church numbered but twelve. Our first object is theological reform; the world, we believe, is ripe for it. We are striving for the reunion of reason and faith, — two principles which God hath joined together, but which man hath long ago divorced. Our purpose is to remove the obstacles which now shut out the Bible from the understanding, the conscience, and the heart of mankind. To effect these objects, numbers are not necessary. Truth is not propagated by armies, though error often is. Truth conquers by her own might. Our mission, at the present moment, requires, not numbers, but wisdom, learning, piety, patience, industry. These things we covet, these things we cultivate and strive to attain. We see no reason for discouragement. Everywhere we see progress, everywhere fresh acknowledgment of the principles we hold dear, and a century of advancement such as the last thirty years have witnessed will bring most religious sects in this country to the ground we occupy.

DISCOURSE II.

UNITARIANS NOT INFIDELS.

BUT WE DESIRE TO HEAR OF THEE WHAT THOU THINKEST: FOR AS CONCERNING THIS SECT, WE KNOW THAT EVERYWHERE IT IS SPOKEN AGAINST. — Acts xxviii. 22.

THE most common accusation made against Unitarians is, that they are *unbelievers*. This is no new charge, as brought by one Christian denomination against another. It is often, and very easily, said, by one controversialist against another, that he is an infidel, or an unbeliever. And the charge generally amounts to this, that one denies what the other believes. Each insists on the particular doctrine which he makes prominent, as the great, central truth of the Gospel, and says, and perhaps thinks, that his opponent, if he denies that, might as well deny the whole Gospel.

This is precisely the case in the present instance. It is said of us, that we do not believe in Christ. This is an equivocal expression. It may mean, that we do not believe that any such person ever lived. It may mean, that we put no confidence in what he said, — that he was not what he pretended to be, or what his disciples afterwards pretended he had been. It may mean, and does probably mean, in the case we are considering, that we do not believe that he was God.

The phraseology is sometimes varied, and it is said that we do not believe in the Divinity of Christ. This, again, is an equivocal expression. It may mean, that his person was divine, or that his words and actions were divine. It may mean that he was Jehovah, the only living and true God. In that case the proper expression would be, that we do not believe in the Deity of Christ.

If Christ was not God, then we may believe in him, and believe in him to the saving of the soul, and still not believe that he was God. The whole question as to what is a true faith in Christ turns upon the question whether he were God or not.

In order to settle this question, we must go to the Scriptures, and inquire what the Apostles believed concerning him. The first convert to belief in Christ was Peter. And what was his confession of faith? According to Matthew, it was, — "Thou art the Christ, the Son of the living God." And what did Peter mean by this? Did he mean to make any assertion concerning the *nature* of Christ, or merely his *office*? The very phrase does not assert, but denies, Deity. A Son of God cannot be God, for three reasons, — because he is derived, because he cannot be eternal, and because he must be separate from God. But so far is the second clause, "the Son of the living God," from making an important part of Peter's confession of faith, that the other two Evangelists who have related this confession, Mark and Luke, have left it out altogether. Mark records that he merely said, "Thou art the Christ"; and Luke, "Thou art the Christ of God." The meaning of the word "Christ" is "anointed." The anointed of God cannot be God. If the second clause, "the Son of the living God," had contained the essence or the most important part of Peter's confession, as relating to the nature of Christ, Mark and Luke certainly would not have left it out. We may safely say, then, that the confession of Peter had no relation to the nature of Christ whatever, but only to his office.

But Peter must be allowed to be the best interpreter of his own language. Peter, after the resurrection of Christ, was sent, by especial commission, to convert Cornelius, and teach him the first principles of the Christian religion ; and the faith which he propounds to Cornelius concerning Christ is this : — "How God anointed Jesus of Nazareth with the Holy Ghost and with power ; who went about doing good, and healing all that were oppressed of the devil : for *God was with him.* And we are witnesses of all things which he did, both in the land of the Jews and in Jerusalem ; whom they slew, and hanged on a tree: *him God raised up* the third day, and showed him openly." The anointing of Jesus of Nazareth with the Holy Ghost and with power did not prove him to be God. It rather proved him not to be God. Had he been God, he would not have needed, nor could he have received, such an anointing. Neither do crucifixion and being raised from the dead agree with the supposition that Christ was God.

Now this is precisely the Unitarian belief concerning Jesus of Nazareth, — that God anointed him with the Holy Ghost and with power, endowed him with that transcendent and unapproachable wisdom which he exhibited, gave him the supernatural knowledge that he possessed, communicated to him the sublime and perfect doctrine that he taught, sealed his mission by the miracles which he performed, and, when the Jews and Romans had murdered him upon the cross, raised him from the dead and showed him to his disciples, that they might be the witnesses of these stupendous events, on which our religion is founded, to that and all succeeding ages.

With what propriety, then, can Unitarians be denounced as unbelievers in Christ, when they believe concerning him the very thing which Peter did, who was blessed by his Master, and called the foundation-stone of the Christian Church? Belief in Christ has nothing to do with his nature, but only with his mission, — whether God did or did not anoint him with the Holy Ghost and with power, did or did not raise him from the dead.

Paul takes the same view of this subject in the fifteenth chapter of First Corinthians : — " If Christ be not risen, then is our preaching vain, and your faith is also vain. Yea, and we are found false witnesses of God, because we have testified of God that he raised up Christ ; whom he raised not up, if so be that the dead rise not." Here, then, the main point of Christian faith is, not that Christ was God, but that God had raised him from the dead. To believe that Christ was God, and that God raised him from the dead, is to believe totally different propositions.

And why was a belief in the resurrection of Christ so important ? Paul tells us, in the first chapter of his Epistle to the Romans : — " Declared to be the Son of God," or the Messiah, " with power, according to the spirit of holiness, *by the resurrection from the dead.*" The resurrection proved nothing as to the nature of Christ. It did demonstrate him to be the Messiah.

It is objected to Unitarians, that they *rely too much on human reason* ; that they set up reason in opposition to Scripture, and in opposition to faith. Let us examine this matter, and see if this charge be just. What is the relation of reason to Scripture and to faith ?

We affirm that the use of reason is necessary to

determine whether the Scriptures are to be received as a divine revelation; and, when they are so received, the use of reason is necessary to find out what they teach; and, in the third place, faith, instead of being opposed to reason, is built upon it.

In the first place, reason is the only means which God has given us of distinguishing what is true from what is false, what is probable from what is improbable, what is to be believed from what is not to be believed. The New Testament is given us, and we read it. There is no way for us to determine whether it is true or false, except by the use of our reason. If we must receive the New Testament merely because it is placed before us, then the Mahometan is just as much compelled to receive the Koran because it is placed before him.

A man says that he receives the New Testament as a Divine revelation. Another asks him, Why? He then goes on to give his *reasons.* He says that the narrative is natural, and bears the marks of truth. That is, it resembles other narratives which he knows to be true. The comparison of that narrative with other narratives is the work of reason, and the inference he draws from it is the work of reason. He says that Paul and Peter and John and the other Apostles would not have consumed their lives, and finally sacrificed them, in testifying to a falsehood. This inference is an act of reason. Faith in the New Testament, then, is built on reason. And if it were not, it would be mere credulity.

In the second place, we must use reason in finding out what the Bible teaches. All sects do this, even those who disclaim reason most vehemently. All sects use it, till it begins to press upon their peculiar doctrines, and then they discard it. The Catholic uses it. He reads in the New Testament the passage in which Christ calls himself a "vine." Is he to receive this literally or figuratively? If he is not allowed to use reason, he must believe that Christ was literally a vine, that he was planted in the earth, and had roots and branches; and the only reason he can give why he does not so receive it is, that it is not *reasonable* to believe that this was Christ's meaning. Upon the strength of reason, he rejects the literal meaning of the words. But when he comes to the passage, "This is my body," he refuses to use his reason, and says that this assertion must be interpreted literally, and he must believe that it was the real flesh of Christ. The Trinitarian Protestant insists on using his reason in the same way, in this case, that the Catholic did in regard to the assertion of Christ that he was a vine. He judges that it is more *reasonable* to believe that Christ meant to say that the bread *represented* his body, as his body was present, unbroken and unchanged.

But there is a limit to his application of reason to the interpretation of Scripture, as well as to that of the Catholic. Christ said, on a certain occasion, —

"I and the Father are one." He insists that this passage must be interpreted literally, that God and Christ are one being. You ask him how two beings can be one being, and he answers, that he does not pretend to explain it. It is a mystery, and must be received, notwithstanding its repugnance to reason. But he would not allow the Catholic to make the same plea in favor of the doctrine of transubstantiation.

The Unitarian goes on to apply reason to the interpretation of this passage also. He inquires if the same writer do not employ the same word in cases in which no identity of being is intended. He reads on a few chapters, and he finds the Saviour praying for his disciples in these words, — "that they all may be one." And in the next verse he specifies the sense in which they were to be one to be the same with that in which he had applied the same expression to himself and God, — "that they may be one, *even as we are.*" If the expression be allowed to prove that God and Christ were numerically one, then the same expression must be allowed to prove that God and Christ and the disciples were all one being.

The only difference, then, that there is between the Unitarian and other Christians is, that he applies reason to the interpretation of *all* the Scriptures, whereas they apply it only to a part. Without the use of reason, revelation would be useless; for we could never know what was revealed and what was not revealed, what was figurative and what literal. If it be meant by placing reason above Scripture, that, when reason and Scripture come in conflict, we believe reason in preference to Scripture, we deny that any such case ever happened, or ever can happen; for we affirm that the Scriptures teach nothing that is not perfectly reasonable, when they are properly interpreted.

Revelation teaches more, and on higher evidence, than reason. If it did not, it would be wholly useless and superfluous. If it added nothing to what we knew before, it could do us no good. Reason teaches the probability of a future life; but the assurance of Christ, and his own resurrection, make it certain. But it is only by the use of reason that we can arrive at the well-grounded conviction, that Christ ever uttered such an assurance, or ever rose from the dead. It is only by the use of reason that the accounts of the supernatural events recorded in the New Testament can be separated and distinguished from the thousand other accounts of supernatural events which have been handed down to us from the past. Accordingly, every book that has ever been written on the evidences of Christianity is a recital of the reasons we have for believing the supernatural accounts of the Old and New Testaments, and rejecting all others. These books are addressed to the reasoning faculty of man. If the reasoning is not satisfactory, the revelation has no authority.

I go further, and say that it is reason only which can give us confidence in a revelation, even when we are convinced that one has been made. The truth of revelation, even when it is made, depends upon the veracity of God, upon the question whether it is probable that he would or would not deceive us. The probability that he would not deceive us depends entirely upon the fact, whether he be a good being. And the only evidence we have that he is a good being is the predominance of good over evil in his works, or of happiness over misery in the creatures he has made. The representation is not true, then, that Unitarians set up reason in opposition to Scripture, and in opposition to faith. They make use of reason for the establishment of Scripture, and for the establishment of faith. They make use of reason for the interpretation of Scripture, that they may ascertain what it teaches and what it does not teach.

It is objected to Unitarians, that they expect to be saved by their own merits, whereas the only ground of salvation is the merits of Christ. Both parts of this objection are founded on misapprehension. There is no such thing mentioned in the Scriptures as being saved by the merits of Christ. There is no such phrase in the Scriptures as "the merits of Christ." There is no intimation that the merits of Christ, whatever they might have been, can by any possibility become the merits of any other person. Merit is a thing which can no more be transferred than personal identity. If merit could be transferred from one person to another, then this world, as a scene of probation, might be dispensed with. Salvation must either be arbitrary or universal. All that would be necessary to be done for the worst of men, when he leaves the world, would be for the merits of Christ to be set to his account, and then his condition would be as good as that of the best. Christ never made mention of any such plan of salvation as this. He made no promise of the transfer of his personal merits to his followers. There is no way in which a bad man can become a good man, except by his personal acts. A bad man cannot become a good man without repentance, which is a personal act. A bad man cannot become a good man without reformation, that is, without obedience. Accordingly, the first word which Christ uttered was, "Repent." In the first sermon he delivered, he pronounced blessings on the humble, the meek, the pure in heart, the merciful, the peacemakers, the persecuted for righteousness' sake, and assured them that the kingdom of heaven was theirs, — that they would be for ever happy. These things were not the merits of Christ. They were all personal qualities, which fitted them for the happiness of heaven. He did not come to substitute reliance on his merits, in the place of obedience to God's law, for final acceptance. "Think not," said he, in the same discourse, "that I am come to destroy the law or the prophets: I am not come to destroy, but to fulfil. For verily I say unto you, Till heaven and earth pass, one jot or one tittle shall in no wise pass from the law, till all be fulfilled. Whosoever, therefore, shall break one of these least commandments, and shall teach men so, he shall be called the least in the kingdom of heaven: but whosoever *shall do* and teach them, the same shall be called great in the kingdom of heaven." Does this look like being saved by the merits of Christ?

The next verse informs us of the nature and degree of that righteousness which was to fit Christ's disciples for the kingdom of heaven. First he tells them of the kind and degree of righteousness which the Scribes and Pharisees thought necessary, and then informs them what he requires:—"I say unto you, that except your righteousness shall exceed the righteousness of the Scribes and Pharisees, ye shall in no case enter into the kingdom of heaven." What was their righteousness? "Ye have heard that it was said by them of old time, Thou shalt not kill; and whosoever shall kill shall be in danger of the judgment. But I say unto you, that whosoever is angry with his brother without a cause shall be in danger of the judgment." "Ye have heard that it hath been said, Thou shalt love thy neighbour, and hate thine enemy. But I say unto you, Love your enemies, bless them that curse you, do good to them that hate you, and pray for them which despitefully use you and persecute you ; that ye may be the children of your Father which is in heaven." Luke reports that he added, — " And your reward shall be great." Your reward for what ? Certainly not for the merits of Christ, but the cultivation and practice of the Christian virtues just enumerated, kindness, forbearance, justice. He winds up this enumeration of Christian virtues by saying, — " Be ye therefore perfect, even as your Father which is in heaven is perfect." Now it cannot be said that God is perfect by any other righteousness except his own, and if man is perfect by Christ's merits, then his perfection is *not* of the same kind with that of God. The perfection of God had just been specified : — " For he maketh his sun to rise on the evil and on the good, and sendeth rain on the just and on the unjust."

After proposing as the laws of his kingdom the whole circle of the most exalted virtues, Christ closes with the following declarations : — " Not every one that saith unto me, Lord, Lord, shall enter into the kingdom of heaven ; but he that *doeth the will* of my Father which is in heaven." " Therefore, whosoever heareth these sayings of mine, *and doeth them*, I will liken him unto a wise man, which built his house upon a rock ; and the rain descended, and the floods came, and the winds blew, and beat upon that house, and it fell not : for it was founded on a rock. And every one that heareth these sayings of mine, and *doeth them not*, shall be likened unto a foolish man, which built his house upon the sand; and the rain descended, and the floods came, and the winds blew, and beat upon that house, and it fell: and great was the fall of it." Nothing is here said of the merits of Christ as a ground of salvation. The reason of acceptance is, not the appropriating of his merits, but doing his commandments. In another place he describes the general judgment, but says nothing of his merits as the ground of discrimination between those on his right hand and on his left. In another place he says, — "They that have *done good* shall come forth unto the resurrection of life, and they that have done evil unto the resurrection of condemnation."

Yet, notwithstanding these representations, no Unitarian believes nor preaches that any man can demand salvation on account of his good works, because his best works are imperfect, and he often sins. For acceptance of his best deeds, he must rely on the benignity of God, for he has done no more than he was bound to do. For the forgiveness of his sins, he must be dependent on God's mercy. But such is God's goodness, that he has no doubt of either.

This brings me to the only remaining charge against Unitarians which I shall have space to notice this evening. It is said of us, that we deny the Atonement. This charge is a difficult one to meet, because of its vagueness. It is difficult to find out what the doctrine of atonement is, that we are accused of denying. There have been almost as many different schemes of atonement as there have been different writers upon the subject. Princeton says one thing, and Andover another. Oberlin proposes another explanation, differing from both.

The first and most common scheme of atonement is, that the sufferings of Christ were designed to appease the wrath of God. God was angry with men on account of the sin of Adam, as well as their own sins. God the Son, the second person of the Trinity, interposed to turn away his wrath, to receive in his own person the inflictions of God's vindictive displeasure, and thus rescue man from it. We do reject this scheme of atonement most distinctly and emphatically. We say that it has no foundation in Scripture, and that it is inconsistent with the nature and character of God. It is, moreover, inconsistent with itself. On the supposition that the doctrine of the Trinity were true, sin is committed against God, the whole Trinity, — against one person as much as another. The second person cannot abandon his place in the Trinity, and come on earth and make atonement to the whole Trinity, because he must be at the same time one of the persons of the Trinity to which the atonement is made. The very supposition upon which this scheme is raised is an impossibility, and therefore requires no further discussion.

The next scheme of atonement which I shall mention may be called "the satisfaction scheme." It is said, that mankind had broken God's law, and thus impaired its authority. If men were pardoned merely on repentance, without the legal penalty being exacted from some one, the law would become a nullity, and no longer have power to control God's creatures. It was necessary that some one should be punished, lest the Deity should lose his dignity and respect. Every sin is an infinite evil, because committed against an infinite God. An infinite atonement is necessary to do away an infinite evil. It was necessary that Christ should be both God and man, in order to make an infinite sacrifice. But, unfortunately for this theory, those who adopt it are compelled to confess that God is incapable of suffering, so that the human part alone suffered, and the infinite atonement is at last explained away. Besides, Christ upon the cross exclaimed, "My God, my God, why hast thou forsaken me?" and with his last breath said, "Father, into thy hands I commend my spirit." If God made a part of his person, he could not have forsaken him. And if he remained to make the infinite atonement, that prayer did not correspond to facts. But this idea of satisfying the law is wholly gratuitous. Nothing is said of it in Scripture.

What, then, is the atonement, and in what sense do Unitarians believe in it? In the first place, I observe that the word is found but once in the New

Testament, and then it is the translation of a Greek word, which everywhere else is rendered *reconciliation*. Had it been here so translated, we should never have heard either of the word or the doctrine of atonement.

The simple facts of the case are these. A disobedient child is always at variance with his father. There can be no reconciliation, or at-one-ment, between them, until the son repents, reforms, and returns humbled and obedient to his father. Such is the condition of those whom Christ endeavoured to reconcile to God. Reconciliation is a voluntary act, and can be brought about only by persuasion. Christ was a teacher. His mission was that of a teacher. His death was the consequence of his teaching, and of his assumption of the office of the Messiah. The faith which he claimed from his disciples had nothing to do with his nature. It was, that he had been sent by God, and instructed and empowered to do what he did, and teach what he taught. That teaching was his principal office, he more than once asserts. "I am come a light into the world, that whosoever believeth on me should not walk in darkness." Belief on him as a teacher was the belief which secured salvation. "Verily, verily, I say unto you, he that heareth my word, and believeth on him that sent me, hath everlasting life, and shall not come into condemnation, but is passed from death unto life." To his disciples he said, *before* his crucifixion, — "*Now* ye are clean, *through the word that I have spoken unto you.*" It was his doctrine, then, not his death, which cleansed his disciples from sin. Indeed, Christ's death without his doctrines could have no influence upon the world, for men cannot be forgiven unless they repent. It is only by bringing men to repentance and obedience, that he can be of any service to them. To reject him as a teacher is to reject him altogether. "He that rejecteth me, and receiveth not my words, hath one that judgeth him; the word that I have spoken, that shall judge him at the last day. For I have not spoken of myself, but the Father, which hath sent me, he gave me a commandment what I should say and what I should speak, and I know that his commandment is life everlasting."

One part of Christ's doctrine was the readiness of God to forgive the penitent. Such is the meaning of the parable of the prodigal son. The doctrine of the forgiveness of sins made a part, and a substantial part, of Christ's teaching; it became a part of the new covenant or dispensation of religion, a part of God's revealed and stipulated way of dealing with men.

In the course of his teaching, Jesus was arraigned by the Jews as guilty of blasphemy, in pretending to be their promised Messiah, and for teaching the people in the name of God. They brought him before their highest court, and the chief priest solemnly interrogated him, — "Art thou the Christ?" Here were his whole mission and ministry brought to the test. If he had shrunk from that avowal, there would have been an end to his mission and his religion. The world at large would never have known that such a person had lived. But he said, "I am," and was ordered to execution. He shed his blood, then, in bearing testimony to his Divine mission; his blood was the seal of the new covenant, a part of which covenant was the promise of God to forgive the penitent. This is what he meant, then, in instituting the Supper, when he took the cup and said, "This is the new covenant in my blood, which is shed for many for the remission of sins." My blood is the seal of that covenant, which promises the forgiveness of sins. This is the sense in which Jesus was "the Lamb of God, which taketh away the sin of the world." The mere pardon of sin is of little consequence, unless at the same time there is a change of character. It would have been of no use for the father to forgive the prodigal son, unless he had repented. If he had come back impenitent, the state of things would not have been improved at all, though the father had forgiven the impenitent son.

Christ is the ambassador of God's mercy to men. He promised them pardon on repentance, and acceptance on the ground of obedience, — reward, even, for every good act. But that embassage is made infinitely more impressive by the crucifixion. That Christ foresaw and foretold : — " And I, if I be lifted up from the earth, will draw all men unto me."

So we find that it is the moral effect of Christ's death *upon us* on which the writers of the New Testament principally dwell, when speaking of the subject. " He suffered, the just for the unjust," — that he might appease the Divine wrath, or vindicate the honor of the law ? — no ; but " that he might bring us unto God." " Who gave himself for us," — that he might expiate our sins ? — no ; but " that he might redeem us from all iniquity, and purify unto himself a peculiar people, zealous of good works." " Forasmuch as ye know that ye were not redeemed by corruptible things, as silver and gold," — from what ? — the wrath of God, the penalties of the law ? — no ; but " from your vain conversation, received by tradition from your fathers," from your vicious habits and practices, which were handed down from preceding generations, " by the precious blood of Christ, as of a lamb without blemish and without spot." Now there is no possible way in which the blood of Christ can reform men from their evil habits, except by giving moral power and efficacy to the Gospel, in persuading men to abandon sin and practise holiness.

Such, then, are the views of Unitarians with respect to the atonement. They do not believe that Christ died to appease God's wrath ; they do not believe that he died to satisfy the claims of the broken law. They *do* believe that he died to give power and efficacy to his Gospel, to fix on him the faith and affections of mankind, that they might be delivered from sin, and be induced to become holy, just, and good ; to break off their sins by righteousness, and their iniquities by turning to God, and thus become reconciled to that Father from whom they were alienated by wicked works.

The Unitarian hopes to be saved, not by his own merits, nor by the merits of Christ, but by the free, unbought, spontaneous mercy of God, of which boundless and unchangeable love the mission and death of Christ are an expression and a manifestation. " For God so loved the world, that he gave his only begotten Son, that whosoever believeth in him should not perish, but have everlasting life."

The atonement, or reconciliation, is not so much a speculative as a practical subject, in which every one is interested who hears me this night. Each one of you knows whether he is reconciled to God or not, or whether he is estranged from him. Christ has told you how you can find peace :— " Come unto me, all ye that labor and are heavy-laden, and I will give you rest. Take my yoke upon you, and *learn* of me ; for I am meek and lowly in heart ; and ye shall find rest to your souls."

DISCOURSE III.

EXPLAINING THE BIBLE AND EXPLAINING IT AWAY

SANCTIFY THEM THROUGH THY TRUTH: THY WORD IS TRUTH. —John xvii. 17.

THE charges against Unitarians which I am this evening to meet and answer are, that they *mutilate* the Scriptures in some instances, and *explain them away* in others, in order to sustain their peculiar doctrines. Sometimes it is said, that we do not use the same Bible which is used by the rest of the Christian world. The impression intended to be conveyed by all these representations is, that the Scriptures are so plainly against us that they must be disposed of in some unfair way before our doctrines can be established, and where a text makes against us, we either deny its genuineness, or put some forced and unnatural construction upon it, to make it square with our faith. It is the object of this discourse to examine and confute these charges, to show that we are more zealous than any other sect for the purity of God's word, that where the accusation can be made against us of straining the words of Scripture from their obvious meaning, the same charge may be made a hundred times as often against those who accuse us; that we are never compelled by our system to explain away the Scriptures, but only to explain them; whereas there is hardly a page in the Bible which Trinitarians are not compelled to explain away.

We begin with the integrity of the text. It is not pretended by the advocates of the Trinity that there is one single text in the Bible in which it is plainly taught. There is no such word as Trinity in the Bible, from beginning to end. Such a word was never coined till many ages after the Bible was written. Both the great Reformers, Luther and Calvin, were dissatisfied with it and disapproved of its use. Luther says, — "The word Trinity sounds oddly, and is a human invention; it were better to call the Almighty, God, than Trinity." Calvin says he has no objection to its being disused, or "buried," and, in another place, — "I like not this prayer, O holy, blessed, and glorious Trinity! it savors of barbarism. The word Trinity is barbarous, insipid, profane, a human invention, grounded on no testimony of the word of God."

The Catholics, the most numerous branch of the Christian Church, do not pretend that the doctrine of the Trinity can be proved from the Scriptures. They confess that it is received by their church on the ground of tradition alone. The Protestants, with singular inconsistency, deny tradition, but hold the doctrine of the Trinity, when the foundation upon which the Catholics rested it is taken away. There is only one text in the Bible which expresses any thing like a Trinity, and that is the seventh verse of the fifth chapter of the First Epistle of John: — "For there are three that bear record in heaven, the Father, the Word, and the Holy Ghost; and these three are one." But this text is spurious, and made no part of the original Epistle of John. All scholars, of all parties and sects, who have examined the evidence, have abandoned this text as making no part of the word of God. Still, it is cited and preached from, as being genuine, by clergymen who ought to be acquainted with this fact. Certainly, under these circumstances, we have a right to retort the charge of irreverence to the sacred Scriptures. It is quite as disrespectful to the Scriptures to attempt to interpolate a passage into them of mere human device, as to expunge a passage that is genuine, which the Unitarians have never done.

The New Testament, as you well know, was written in the Greek language, and we have manuscripts of it written more than a thousand years ago. We have translations made from it still earlier into various languages. This verse is not found in any one of them It is needless to add, that its reception cannot be sustained for a moment. And it seems to be a fact ominous to the cause of Trinitarianism, that the only text to which it can appeal as direct testimony turns out to be a manifest interpolation. How can it be justified for a moment, that a minister of God's truth should stand up and quote this text in proof of the Trinity, without giving any intimation of its being an interpolation?

There is another passage which is often quoted in the Trinitarian controversy, to which no weight ought to be attached. It is found in First Timothy, third chapter, sixteenth verse: — "Great is the mystery of godliness: God was manifest in the flesh, justified in the spirit, seen of angels, preached unto the Gentiles, believed on in the world, received up in glory." There are no less than three variations of the ancient manuscripts, on which most reliance is placed in settling the text of the New Testament. One reading is, — "He who was manifested in the flesh was justified in the spirit." Another, — "Great is the mystery of godliness, which was manifested in the flesh." The other is the common reading. "God was manifested in the flesh." The whole Catholic Church, throughout the world, knows no other reading than "Great is the mystery of godliness, which was manifested in the flesh," as any of you may easily ascertain by examining a Catholic Bible at the place referred to. Sir Isaac Newton, one of the best as well as most learned of men, wrote a distinct treatise to show that the common reading — "God was manifested in the flesh" — is a corruption of the text, and was unknown in the churches for the first three hundred years. By the best critics, this reading is rejected, and no honest man, who knows the whole ground, will ever quote this text as having any bearing on the Trinitarian controversy, or quote it at all without noticing the fact, that the reading is so doubtful, that no argument ought to be drawn from it.

There is another passage which is situated in the same way. It is found in the twentieth chapter, twenty-eighth verse, of Acts: — "Feed the church of God, which he hath purchased with his own blood." This reading is of modern origin. The true reading, according to the most ancient manuscripts, is, — "Feed the church of the Lord, which he hath purchased with his own blood," — referring, of course, to Christ.

These three passages of the New Testament are admitted, by the best critical scholars, to be corruptions of the text. All honest men ought to unite in giving them their true character. No honest scholar can allow them to be quoted as of any authority in the Trinitarian controversy. If the doctrine of the Trinity were anywhere plainly taught, then an argument might be allowed some force which was itself doubtful. But to sustain a doubtful doctrine by a text which is itself of doubtful authority, is by no means to be allowed.

We do not mutilate the Scripture, then, when we

insist that these texts shall be set aside. We are doing all that in us lies to restore it to its primitive integrity.

We now come to the second charge, that we *explain away* those passages which we do not deny and expunge. That is to say, we put a forced construction on them, and depart from their natural meaning to a degree wholly unjustifiable. Let us examine this matter carefully, and see how it stands.

In the first place, I would observe that the Unitarian has very little to explain away. It is not pretended that there is a single text in the Bible in which the doctrine of the Trinity is plainly taught. The Unitarian, then, can have but very little that is really difficult to explain away. It is not pretended that the Trinity is any thing other than a doctrine of *inference*. An inference may be a mistaken inference, and it is a very different thing to explain away an inference from explaining away a plain, direct, and positive declaration.

Let us try two or three of the strongest Trinitarian texts. The benediction at the close of the Second Epistle to the Corinthians has always been considered as containing one of the strongest arguments for the Trinity: — "The grace of the Lord Jesus Christ, the love of God, and the communion of the Holy Ghost be with you all." Here, it is said, there are the three persons of the Trinity brought together, and a blessing implored from each of them.

In the first place, we observe, that the order is wrong. The Lord Jesus Christ is put first. He is thought to be the second person of the Trinity. And the second person of this Trinity is God, the whole Deity. "The love of God." God, the whole Deity, cannot be a person of the Trinity. If the second person of this Trinity is God, the whole Deity, and is connected with Christ and the Holy Ghost by the particle "*and*," Christ and the Holy Ghost cannot be God at all, by the very terms of the proposition. Instead, then, of being one of the strongest arguments *for* the Trinity, this passage, when analyzed, is found to be one of the strongest arguments *against* it. Had the language been, "the love of the Father," then the second clause might have designated a person of the Trinity, according to that hypothesis; but being God, the whole Deity, the second person excludes the other persons, or whatever you may call them, from the Deity altogether.

In giving this analysis, you perceive, we do not explain away the Scripture, — we simply explain it, and show its true meaning; and, in doing so, we explain away the argument which it is thought to contain in favor of the Trinity.

Let us now take up the introduction to the Gospel of John. "In the beginning was the Word, and the Word was with God, and the Word was God. The same was in the beginning with God." This is considered as one of the principal proof-texts of the Trinity, which the Unitarian must use much ingenuity to explain away. But it teaches no Trinity. The word "God" occurs three times in it, but with no intimation of any plurality in the Divine nature. The word "God" comprehends here, as it does in other cases, the whole Deity. What, then, is affirmed? That the Word was with God and was God. The first question to settle is, Is the Word represented as a person? "The Word" is not a proper name, not the name of a person, but of a thing. But let us understand it as a person, the second person of the Trinity. "In the beginning was the second person of the Trinity, and the second person of the Trinity was with God, and the second person of the Trinity was God." This becomes a contradiction in terms. The second person of the Trinity could not be *with* God, for he must then have been a person of the very God with whom he was. The very words of this passage, then, instead of sustaining the doctrine of the Trinity, contradict it. There is no Trinitarian argument, therefore, in the passage to explain away.

In order to understand it, we must find out what is meant by the term "Word." How is God represented as making the world? By his word. He said, — "Let there be light, and there was light." But a little reflection will convince us that this is a figurative expression. Literally interpreted, it would teach that God spoke through human organs, which would involve the supposition that God is material. Commands are addressed to human or intelligent beings, and not to inanimate matter. The Scripture does not mean to say that God created the universe by speaking, when it says, — " By the word of the Lord were the heavens made, and all the host of them by the breath of his mouth " ; but merely to represent the exertion of God's creative power under a human similitude. The term " Word," therefore, represents those *attributes* of God which were exerted in the creation, his wisdom and power. Through them God created the world. By the " Word," then, in this sense of God's wisdom and power, which after all are nothing else or different from God himself, all things were made.

The same attributes of wisdom and power gave being to the human soul, and when it was created gave it intelligence and will. " In it was life, and the life was the light of men." The same sense is expressed in other words : — " The inspiration of the Almighty hath given him understanding." It was the same which gave inspiration to the prophets of the Old Testament. But it was especially manifest in Jesus Christ, inasmuch that in him it became incarnate. Divine power and wisdom came and *dwelt* among us in human form. Such full communications of Divine power and wisdom did Jesus enjoy, that he seemed to the beholders to be the peculiar favorite of Heaven, to be in such favor as an only son is with his father. And he made as much more perfect a revelation to men, as his communion with God seemed more near and intimate, — "For the law was given by Moses, but grace and truth came by Jesus Christ." That there was no personal manifestation of God appears by what comes after. "No man hath *seen* God at any time. The only begotten Son, who is in the bosom of the Father, he hath declared him."

"God" and "Father" are here used as synonymous expressions. To be in the bosom of another is not to share his nature, but his confidence. The Son, as the second person of the Trinity, could not derive his superior knowledge of God from the fact that he was in the bosom of God, for he must have been that very God in whose bosom he was. There is no Trinitarianism, then, in this passage. It is not said that God is three in any sense. The term "Father" is used as applied to God, and it means, not a person of a trinity, but the whole Deity, and is synonymous with the word "God." The term "Son" is applied to Christ, but not as a person of the Trinity, but as a person deriving superior knowledge of God from the fulness of the communications which he had received from the whole Deity. All that is asserted in it, when analyzed, amounts to this, — that, through Christ, God made the most perfect revelation of himself that had ever been given to man, more perfect than in physical nature, more perfect than in the human soul, and more perfect than in the Mosaic dispensation.

This is the natural exposition of the whole passage, when considered part by part. This is explaining Scripture, not explaining it away. Any other explanation introduces confusion into theology and into humanity, besides being forced upon the language of the Scriptures.

Another passage, which is thought most explicitly to teach the Trinity, is the form of baptism. Baptizing them "in the name," or rather into the name, "of the Father, and of the Son, and of the Holy Ghost." Here at least, it is said, are the three persons of the Trinity made all equal, and the disciples are commanded to be baptized into the name of them all. Here is a trinity asserted, and no amount of ingenuity can explain it away. But you note that it is not asserted that each one of these is God, or that they all three are one God. There is, then, no trinity of persons asserted, and of course there is none to explain away. The doctrine of the Trinity is an inference, then, as far as this passage is concerned, and it is a human, fallible inference, and may not be a true inference.

Baptism, in the time of Christ and his Apostles, was a form of public profession. John's baptism was a baptism into repentance, or a profession of repentance, in anticipation of the advent of Christ. To be baptized into Christ, or into Christianity, was to be baptized into a profession of belief in Jesus as the true Messiah. Such was the case with the Jews In their baptism, it is not probable that any more than the name of Jesus was used, as Peter says to them, on the day of Pentecost, — "Repent and be baptized every one of you, *in the name of Jesus Christ*, for the remission of sins, and ye shall receive the gift of the Holy Ghost. Then they which gladly received the word were baptized."

Now, if we consider the form of baptism to relate entirely to the Divine nature, to what will it amount? That God exists in three persons, that one of these persons is son to the other, and the other person is called the Holy Ghost. The form of baptism, under this view of it, is a mere abstract proposition, as to the mode of the Divine existence. It has no relation to the Christian religion, nor to our salvation. It is a mere metaphysical theory, and a theory itself embarrassed with insuperable difficulties.

But interpreting the sonship of Christ of his *office*, his being sent of God, and the Holy Ghost as the seal of his mission, then the form of baptism becomes significant. It becomes a declaration of belief in God as the true God, in Jesus as having been sent and commissioned by him to promulgate and establish Christianity, and in those miraculous events ascribed to the Holy Ghost, by which Christianity was established in the earth.

To this exposition there are no metaphysical objections, no mysterious and incomprehensible Trinity in Unity, and Unity in Trinity. It explains the Bible, and does not explain it away; for it is not pretended that the doctrine of the Trinity is positively asserted, or that it is any thing more than an inference from the form of baptism. If the doctrine of the Trinity were anywhere plainly asserted, then an objection might lie against Unitarianism as explaining away the Bible. All it has to do is to explain away an inference which fallible men have drawn from certain parts of the Scriptures, and which inference in itself involves inconsistencies and contradictions.

Perhaps the nearest approach which the Unitarian makes to being obnoxious to the charge of explaining away the Scriptures is in his exposition of Thomas's exclamation, recorded in the twentieth chapter of John. "And Thomas answered and said unto him, My Lord and my God." Here the appellation "God" is applied to Christ. The question between the Unitarian and the Trinitarian is, What did Thomas mean by it? Did he mean to recognize Jesus as the Jehovah of the Jews, the Creator and Sovereign of the universe? or did he mean to apply the appellation "God" to him as the Jews did the same appellation to kings and magistrates, as a title of the highest respect? or was it merely an exclamation of surprise which escaped his lips in a moment of sudden transport, and not intended as a logical affirmation of any proposition in regard to Christ's nature?

Most Unitarians adopt the second explanation. The word "God" in the Bible is not exclusively appropriated to Jehovah. It is likewise applied to kings and magistrates. "God standeth in the congregation of the mighty, he judgeth among the Gods. How long will ye judge unjustly, and accept the persons of the wicked?" "I have said, Ye are Gods, and all of you are children of the Most High. But ye shall die like men, and perish like one of the people." In a psalm composed in honor of one of the reigning monarchs of Israel, the writer speaks thus:— "My heart is indicting a good matter: I speak of the things which I have made touching *the king:* my tongue is the pen of a ready writer. Thou art fairer than the children of men: grace is poured into thy lips: therefore God hath blessed thee for ever." "Thy throne, O God, is for ever and ever, the sceptre of thy kingdom is a right sceptre. Thou lovest righteousness, and hatest wickedness; therefore God, even thy God, hath anointed thee with the oil of gladness above thy fellows." This passage is quoted in the Epistle to the Hebrews and applied to Christ. It must be applied to Christ, then, not in his divine nature, but his Messianic dignity, for in it is contained this expression:—"Therefore God, even *thy* God, hath anointed thee with the oil of gladness above thy fellows." Christ, in his divine nature, cannot have a God, cannot be exalted, cannot have fellows.

Thomas, then, may have applied the epithet

"God" to Christ in the same sense, not meaning to address him as Jehovah, but as one whom Jehovah had exalted to the highest dignity.

The circumstances which determine my mind to this interpretation are these. The point at issue between Thomas and his fellow-disciples was not the Deity of Jesus, but whether he were risen from the dead. "But Thomas, one of the twelve, was not with them when Jesus came. The other disciples, therefore, said unto him, We have seen the Lord." That the disciples had seen Jesus was no evidence that he was Jehovah, "whom no man hath seen, or can see," but only that he had risen from the dead. "But he said unto them, Except I shall see in his hands the print of the nails, and thrust my hand into his side, I will not believe." This evidence was given him. He saw and felt, he had the concurrent testimony of two of his senses, — to what? that Jesus was Jehovah? — Jehovah can neither be touched nor seen; — no; but that Jesus was risen from the dead, and of consequence must be the true Messiah. His words, then, are to be interpreted as an exclamation of satisfaction as to the point upon which he had doubted, that his Master was risen from the dead. And putting any meaning upon this passage, it does not assert that God is three in any sense, and leaves the Unitarian nothing to explain away.

What John, who was a witness to this transaction,

considered to be proved by it, is evident from the next verse but one : — " And many other signs truly did Jesus in the presence of his disciples, which are not written in this book. But these are written, that ye might believe," — what ? — that Jesus is God ? — no ; but " that Jesus is the Christ, the Son of God, and that believing ye might have life through his name." To believe in Jesus as the Christ is to believe, not that he is God, but the anointed of God. The phrase " Son of God," is merely a synonyme for " Messiah."

But the Trinitarian has an infinitely harder task before him. He has something to explain away. The doctrine of the unity of God is not a doctrine of inference. It is directly asserted over and over, and there is scarcely a page of the Bible on which it is not either expressed or taken for granted. The Trinitarian, in order to sustain his creed, has all these texts, not only to explain, but to explain away.

The word " God " occurs more than two thousand times in the Old Testament, and nowhere with any intimations of a trinity of persons in his nature. All these texts are arguments for the unity of God, and must by the Trinitarian be explained away. One of the chief precepts written down in the book of the law was, — " Jehovah, our God, Jehovah is one." Here is a positive affirmation of the unity of God, in the most absolute sense. This is not only to be explained, but explained away. And the explanation that is usually given of it is, that it is not intended to contradict the idea that there may be three persons in God, but only that there is one God, in opposition to the many gods of the heathen.

But there is another text, indeed, many other texts, in which a trinity of persons is equally contradicted. In the bush, God gives his name as "I Am," and tells Moses to say to the children of Israel, "I Am hath sent me." If there were three persons in God, is there any possible way in which the God of truth could have so effectually misled Moses and the Israelites as to the unity or plurality of the Divine nature, if he really were a trinity of persons, as in the use of such language as this, designating his very essence by the name, "I Am"? Accordingly, neither Moses nor the Jews ever had the least conception of a trinity of persons in God, from that day to this.

We now come down to the New Testament. Did Jesus teach any new doctrine with respect to the Divine nature? He made the unity of God the foundation-stone of his religion, as Moses had done of his. He quotes the very words of Moses: — "The first of all the commandments is, Jehovah, your God, Jehovah is one." This passage must not only be explained, but explained away, before there can be any room to prove the Trinity. Here is a positive assertion, by Christ himself, of the unity of God. To explain away a positive assertion is a very different thing from explaining away a mere inference.

Christ prayed, and often. But then, to explain that recorded fact, it is said that he prayed in his human nature. We answer, that it is mere assumption to imagine that he had two natures. Such a fact is nowhere stated in the Bible, and cannot be assumed till it is proved. But if he taught a trinity, and knew that a trinity existed, if he prayed in his human nature, he ought to have prayed to a trinity. But he never prayed to a trinity.

In order to make the Bible bear a Trinitarian explanation, another hypothesis is invented, that the word "Father," when applied to God, sometimes means the first person of a trinity, and sometimes the whole Deity. But that hypothesis, too, ought first to be proved before it is used. At least, one passage ought to be shown in which the word "Father" means the first person of a trinity, for the moment it is allowed that the words "God" and "Father" are coextensive in the New Testament, the doctrine of the Trinity is abandoned. Let us try a few passages. To the woman of Samaria Christ said, — "The hour cometh, and now is, when the true worshippers shall worship THE FATHER in spirit and in truth. GOD is a spirit, and they that worship him must worship him in spirit and in truth." Here "God" and "Father" are used as equal and coextensive terms. If the term "Father" be taken to mean the first person of a trinity, then it would follow that the first person only is an object of worship. "No man hath seen GOD at any time. The only begotten Son, who is in the bosom of THE FATHER, he hath declared him." Here the word "him" refers to God, whom no one hath seen, and "Father" is coextensive with "God." The second person of a trinity cannot be in the bosom of the first, and thus derive his knowledge from him, for they are equal and the same. Such phraseology as this, so far from being an argument in favor of the Trinity, and requiring of the Unitarian to be explained away, contains a strong argument for the unity of God, and therefore must be explained away by the Trinitarian before his hypothesis can be received.

The Lord's prayer contains a strong argument for the Unitarian faith: — "Our Father which art in heaven." "Father" here either stands for the whole Deity, or it authorizes us to worship only the first person of the Trinity. If it is conceded that it comprehends the whole Deity, then it must be admitted, that in order to sustain the doctrine of the Trinity, the meaning of the term "Father" must be shifted to meet circumstances, — sometimes be taken to mean the first person of a trinity, and sometimes the whole Deity. Such a mode of interpretation does not suit the dignity of the word of God. With these considerations in our minds, let us go to

Christ's last prayer with his disciples : — " Father, the hour is come ; glorify thy Son, that thy Son also may glorify thee. As thou hast given him power over all flesh, that he should give eternal life to as many as thou hast given him. And this is life eternal, that they might know thee, *the only true God*, and Jesus Christ whom thou hast sent." Here there can be no doubt that the term " Father " embraces the whole Deity, for he calls him " the only true God." If the Father is the only true God, then the term " Father " either includes the Son and Holy Ghost, or shuts them out of Deity altogether. Christ prayed either in his human or his divine nature. If he prayed in his divine nature, then his divine nature was not God ; for he prays to the only true God *to glorify him with the glory that he had with him before the world was.* One equal person of a trinity could not have received glory from the only true God before the world was. If he did not pray in his divine nature, he prayed in his human nature, and applied the term " Son " to his human nature : — " Glorify thy Son," — afterwards, " Glorify me." If the title " Son " is applied to his human nature here, it may be in every case, and thus be no argument for the Trinity anywhere. If the term " Father," when applied to God, here embraces the whole Deity, it may in every case, and the doctrine of the Trinity falls in pieces by the simple analysis of the terms in which it is expressed.

So in this case, as in every other, the Unitarian is not obliged to explain away the Bible, but only to explain it, and that very explanation explains away the Trinity.

There are hosts of passages equally strong. "There is one God, and one mediator between God and men, the man Christ Jesus." It is impossible to explain this away. "Blessed be *the God* and Father of our Lord Jesus Christ." A person of the Trinity cannot have a God. But this passage affirms that the Lord Jesus Christ not only has a Father, but a God.

Another is found in the first chapter of the Apocalypse: — "The revelation of Jesus Christ, which God gave unto him." The advocates of the Trinity have never been able to give a satisfactory exposition of this passage. There are two difficulties, either of which is insurmountable. One is, that this revelation is represented as having been given to Christ years after his ascension and exaltation to heaven. If Christ were God, or an equal person of the Trinity, no such revelation could possibly have been made to him, for he must have been essentially omniscient.

The other difficulty is, that the revelation is made to Jesus Christ by God; not by the Father, but by God, the whole Trinity. Jesus Christ, then, is shut out of Deity, both by the facts related and by the language used; by his receiving a revelation at all, and his receiving it from GOD, the undivided Deity. Here the usual resort to the distinction between the human and divine nature of Christ will not avail. Professor Stuart of Andover tells us that Christ, though exalted to heaven, will be a dependent being in his mediatorial capacity till the consummation of all things. But this, to my mind, is no explanation how omniscience can be assumed and laid aside at pleasure, or can be conferred and recalled, since it must be an essential and inherent attribute, or not be possessed at all.

There is another passage, which has given the defenders of the Trinity greater trouble, and has never yet found a satisfactory solution. It is found in the thirteenth chapter of Mark: — "But of that day and that hour knoweth no man, no, not the angels which are in heaven, neither the Son, but the Father only." Here omniscience is expressly denied of the "Son." Without some explanation, this passage is fatal to the doctrine of the Trinity, and to the Deity of Christ. In order to evade the force of it, Trinitarians give two explanations. One is, that Christ says this of his human nature, and does not mean to deny omniscience to his divine nature. This, however, would bear hard on his veracity and plain-dealing. It would admit that the title "Son," when used of Christ in connection with the title "Father" when applied to God, means nothing more than his human nature. And this would greatly weaken the force of the argument derived from the form of baptism, — "Baptizing them in the name of the Father, and of the Son," &c. That it is applied to him in his highest capacity, would seem to be intimated by the climax, in which Christ is put between the angels in heaven and God.

The other exposition is, that Christ did not know when the day of judgment or the destruction of Jerusalem was to be, in the sense of not being commissioned to make it known. But philologists have sought in vain, in all Greek literature, for a single instance of the use of the word here rendered "knoweth" with any such meaning. This text, therefore, must remain as it is, wholly incapable of any explanation consistent with the doctrine of the Trinity. It cannot be explained away.

I trust that I have now sufficiently answered the charge made against Unitarians, of mutilating and explaining away the Scriptures. I have shown that the Unitarian has very little to explain away. The Trinitarian, on the other hand, has the current language of the Bible against him, and many passages of which no satisfactory explanation has ever been given.

DISCOURSE IV.

UNITARIANISM NOT MERE MORALITY.

THEREFORE ALL THINGS WHATSOEVER YE WOULD THAT MEN SHOULD DO TO YOU, DO YE EVEN SO TO THEM; FOR THIS IS THE LAW AND THE PROPHETS. — Matthew vii. 12.

IT is often said of Unitarian ministers, that they preach *mere morality*. After hearing a sermon, modelled as near as the best intentions can make it upon the Sermon on the Mount, the Orthodox hearer goes away and says, — "That was a very good moral discourse, but there was no religion in it." So it is said of Unitarians as a class, that they are very good *moral* people, but they have no religion. To my mind, there is no slight praise in such censure as this. In order to censure us, our critics are compelled to reverse the rule of the Saviour. He has given us the rule of judgment in these terms: — "By their fruits ye shall know them. A corrupt tree *cannot* bring forth good fruit." But here the fruit is acknowledged to be good, yet the tree is condemned as corrupt.

But let us take up and examine the charge of

preaching mere morality. What *is* mere morality? Perhaps the principle of mere morality may be summed up in a single sentence, — "Honesty is the best policy." An enlightened regard to self-interest prescribes a course of strict morality. In short, that which is right is to be practised, not because it is right, but because it is expedient. A man must not steal, because the probability is that his theft will be discovered. A man must not lie, because he is sure to be detected, and fall into disgrace. He must not plunge into sensuality, for fear of injuring his health, or wasting his substance. He must not oppress the poor and the dependent, for fear of getting their ill-will, and becoming unpopular. A preacher who should appeal to such motives, and advocate such principles, would preach mere morality.

But this charge is intended to go further. It is intended to *deny*, as well as affirm. It is intended to assert that we do not preach the necessity of a *religious faith* as the *basis* of moral principle and as the basis of moral conduct. It is intended to deny that we lay any stress on *religious emotion*, and to insinuate that we pass it over as enthusiasm and fanaticism. It is intended to deny that we recognize as important *religious experience*, that we regard all spiritual renovation as a delusion, and the growing peace and happiness of a righteous man as a superstitious fancy.

I pronounce all these charges to be wholly and utterly false. In the first place, we assemble in a church. It would not be requisite for us to have churches in order to preach mere morality. A lecture-room would be more appropriate for that purpose. To preach mere morality is to teach philosophy, and the professor's chair is the proper place for that species of instruction. We assemble in a church. And what *is* a church? It is a place of worship, devoutly consecrated and set apart for the services of religion, by solemn prayer and dedicatory rites. It is called, and felt by us to be, "none other than the house of God, and the gate of heaven." Dedicated to God, and consecrated to religious purposes, our religious regard and veneration for the place are expressed, not in words, but in actions, which speak louder, and are more to be believed, — by the decorum, the silence, the reverential respect, which is manifested here. Is *this* mere morality? Is this negation of all religious sentiment and emotion? This deportment, which is spontaneous and unstudied, is the best possible demonstration that we do *not* come here for the purpose of hearing a mere moral lecture, based upon selfish calculation and a heartless, worldly expediency; that we do not fall behind our fellow-Christians of other names in hearty reverence for sacred things.

Here we worship God. Not only are we awed by an especial sense of his presence, but we take his great name upon our lips, we lift up our thoughts to the contemplation of his Divine perfections. We adore him as the Almighty Creator of heaven and earth, as the High and Mighty Ruler of the universe, as the Holy One who inhabiteth eternity, in whose sight the heavens are not clean, and the angels chargeable with folly. We worship him as the Former of our bodies and the Father of our spirits; as the Supreme Lawgiver, whose own finger hath written his statutes in the tablet of our hearts; as the ever-present Witness, to whom all hearts are open and all secrets are known, who cannot be deceived, and will not be mocked; as the Omnipotent and Eternal Rewarder, whose presence is universal and his administration without end, and who will, therefore, bring every work into judgment, with every secret thing, whether it be good or whether it be evil.

Is *this* the administration of mere morality, which has no regard to God or his moral government of the universe?

Here we sing God's praise, in hymns, for the most part, composed by those who entertain theological opinions similar to our own, or by those who differ from us in some particulars of faith, but whose sentiments on subjects in which their opinions and ours coincide we do not hesitate to adopt. Can any human being, without invading the prerogative of Omniscience, take it upon himself to decide, that this part of our worship is a mere formality, that no emotion of our hearts accompanies the song of thanksgiving, the confession of penitence, the avowal of confidence and trust?

Here the Scriptures are read, and carefully separated from all other books, and placed infinitely above them in authority and respect. They are acknowledged as containing the record of a revelation from God. Infinite pains are taken to find out their meaning, to illustrate them by ancient monuments and by contemporaneous history. To them the ultimate appeal is made, when we would ascertain what is the mind and will of God. Especially do we acknowledge the New Testament as the foundation of our religion. All our religious usages are founded on the facts which it relates. The reason why we suspend our worldly avocations and assemble in our churches on the first day of the week is, that the New Testament records the fact, that on that day Jesus Christ, "the author and finisher of our faith," rose from the dead and ascended to heaven. If we did not believe this fact, we should pursue our customary employments. That fact to us puts the seal of God's truth on all that he has taught us. That fact makes the Gospel to us to be, in a manner, the voice of Christ, now speaking to us from the invisible world, from the exaltation to which he is raised, and which in Oriental figure is expressed by his being seated at the right hand of the throne of God.

We baptize our children in his name, together with the name of God and the Holy Ghost, and by that rite we express our obligation to baptize their souls with his truth, early to imbue their minds with the principles of his religion, by precept and by example to train them up to be his true disciples here, that they and we may be partakers of his glory hereafter.

Would not all this be absurd, if we believed and practised nothing but a worldly morality, and are kept within the bounds of decency only by the maxim of earthly wisdom, that honesty is the best policy ?

We celebrate the communion of the Lord's Supper. How can we do this without religious faith, when all that gives the rite any interest or significance to us is the relation which Christ sustains to us as the Ambassador of God's mercy, the Revealer of his will, the faithful and true Witness, and our Forerunner into heaven ? Did we not believe in him in these official capacities, the Lord's Supper would be a mockery, unmeaning and superfluous, and it would be soon abandoned. It is because his doctrine to us is the bread that came down from heaven, of which if a man eat he shall live for ever, which he died on the cross to give us, that the Eucharist has the power to move our religious affections. It is because his blood is the seal of the New Covenant, in which God stipulates to pardon the penitent, and restore them to his favor, that the cup of thanksgiving has to us any interest or signification. It is because the Lord's Supper is a communion with the living and the dead, the Church Universal on earth and in heaven, that it draws us towards it as a sacred ceremony, and gives it a spritual power to sanctify, strengthen, and console us. Could such a rite be perpetuated among us if we had neither religious faith nor feeling, and all our real religion amounted to nothing more than the calculating prudence, that honesty is the best policy? Such conduct would be wholly inexplicable.

But this charge is intended to reach farther, and to throw upon us the odium of denying the reality, the value, and validity of religious experience. Let us examine this charge, and see if it be just.

In the first place, the very fact of preaching to make men better recognizes a difference between a bad man and a good man, and the fact that both the bad man and the good man are sensible of this difference. This consciousness is religious experience. No man from a bad man can become a good man without religious experience. The means we recommend him to use, in order to become a good man, are religious means. We tell him that the shortest way to morality is through religion, and the only sure foundation for morality is religion. If a man becomes truly religious, his morality will take care of itself. But we tell him, too, that, unless his morality keep pace with his religion, he is liable to the grossest self-deception. John the Baptist must first come with his baptism of repentance and reformation, before Jesus can come with his Gospel of holiness and sanctification. Sin we believe to be a disease, to the cure of which abstinence and regimen are as necessary as medicine. Any relapse into old habits nullifies all the effects of medicine, and renders recovery impossible.

We believe in the efficacy of prayer. We believe that it is the most powerful agency that is brought to bear upon the soul of man. We believe that in true prayer the soul opens itself to the influx of Divine influence, just as the upturned flower drinks in the vivifying rays of light and heat from the sun. We believe that God always gives his holy spirit to them that ask it. But we believe, too, that right moral dispositions are necessary to the truth, the reality, and, of consequence, the efficacy of prayer. We believe that the prayers of the wicked are an abomination in the sight of God. We believe that, if we regard iniquity in our hearts, the Lord will not hear our prayer. This is as true of those who reckon themselves among the saints, as of those who acknowledge themselves among the sinners. True repentance is necessary to forgiveness. Reformation is the only sure proof of repentance. "If thou bring thy gift to the altar, and there rememberest that thy brother hath aught against thee, leave there thy gift before the altar, and go thy way; first be reconciled to thy brother, and then come and offer thy gift." We believe in such sort of religious experience as this.

We believe in the efficacy of prayer, but not only

must prayer be offered with right moral dispositions, but directed to proper and legitimate objects. There is no power in prayer to compel God to do what is not in the order of his providence, or to induce him to do that for us which he has made it our duty to do for ourselves. We cannot cause a harvest to spring out of the earth, merely by praying for it. We must till the soil and cast in the seed, and then we may legitimately ask the blessing of God on our labors. So we pray, "Give us day by day our daily bread"; but we do not expect that God will give it to us without labor. If we are reasonable beings, we ask his blessing to prosper our labors. So the Christian prays that he may know the truth, but, if he understands the nature of prayer, he does not expect that God will communicate to him that knowledge by immediate revelation, without study or examination. So he prays to God that he may subdue his evil propensities, but not without his own efforts to do so. We believe that God grants the prayers of his children, just as far as he sees it to be for their good. Is *this* preaching mere morality? Is this denying religious experience?

We admit that our estimate of morality may be different from that of our fellow-Christians, and may be higher. When we look around us, and perceive that the want of common honesty is one of the sorest, if not the very worst, of the evils by which our country is at this moment afflicted, and find that it extends not alone to those who profess to be governed by nothing higher than a mere worldly morality, but to the so-called religious, and that this sad deficiency is sometimes found in the management of religious affairs, and that some of the most fatal and ruinous disgusts to all religion are taken from the detection of the want of moral principle in those who make the loudest religious pretensions, we are sometimes tempted to subscribe to the common sentiment, — "An honest man 's the noblest work of God." We may at least be permitted to place integrity at the foundation of all human excellence.

We do differ somewhat from some Christians in our estimate of the relation which morality bears to God. We believe that the law of morality is God's law, — those conceptions of right and wrong which God has written on the human heart. If conscience is God's law, then obedience to conscience is obedience to God, and in so far is a religious act, even if no especial thought of God comes into the mind. Disobedience to conscience is sin, and sin, from its very nature, is an irreligious act, a violation of religious obligation. If disobedience to conscience be sin, then obedience to conscience must be virtue, and acceptable in the sight of God, or the ways of God are not equal, and his government is a tyranny. If, when the choice is presented to me to do wrong or right, and it is counted sin to me if I do wrong, and not counted a merit if I do right, then I affirm that I am not placed in a condition of fair moral probation.

It may be affirmed, that the highest and purest condition of the soul, the sublimest virtue, is that action in which the soul chooses that which is right merely because it *is* right, without hope of reward or fear of punishment. The very best persons in the world, perhaps, are those who are least conscious of their excellence. Most significantly is it mentioned by Christ, that it is a matter of surprise to the righteous, at the judgment-day, to find themselves commended and welcomed to eternal joy. "Then shall the righteous answer him, saying, *When* saw we thee hungry and fed thee, or thirsty and gave thee drink ?"

Goodness is like health, the highest and most robust states of it are attended with a blessed unconsciousness. It is not a good sign to be always feeling the pulse of one's own moral health. It is not a sign of spiritual soundness. All religious men have religious experience, but the best and the wisest talk the least about it. It is dangerous to talk about it, as it is for us to be over-anxious in inquiring into the condition of the physical system. There is but one Being to whom we are capable of revealing our whole hearts, and he knows them already, and needs not that we unveil them before him. There are some persons whom religious experience, as it is called, seems to injure, instead of benefiting. They were excellent before, in spontaneously obeying the law written upon the heart. But under the influence of religious experience, as it is technically denominated, they become conceited, self-righteous, overbearing, censorious, pharisaical, and lose the virtues of simplicity, candor, kindness, and charity, and gain nothing in their place but sanctimony and spiritual pride.

If Unitarians have erred in laying too little stress upon religious experience, and looking with too much distrust on the results of religious excitements, they have been driven into it by the disgusting cant and pretension they have witnessed in those whose only claim to respect is the vileness of the moral condition from which they profess to have emerged.

Finally, this distinction between morality and religion is not found in the Bible. It is the creation of modern, technical, sectarian theology. It came in with the doctrine of the inherent, constitutional corruption of human nature, which supposes the soul to be alienated from God from the very first, and to require to be created anew by a fiat of his omnipotence before it can possess the *faculties* which are necessary to moral probation, the freedom to choose between good and evil, and an equal disposition towards both.

The Bible recognizes no such ruin and corruption of the human constitution. It regards every human soul as an emanation from the Divinity. As it was at first his workmanship, so it is never forsaken by him.

It is by his continual inspiration that it has understanding. Conscience is nothing other than his voice speaking in the soul of man. The moral nature of man is itself a revelation of God and his will. By it, God holds continual intercourse with all mankind, and puts them in a state of probation, whether they will or will not obey his voice thus speaking within them. This moral discipline extends to the lone savage of the desert, as well as to the enlightened disciple of the revelation he has made through Jesus Christ.

By this universal law, every human being is put on probation every day and hour of his life. His character for good or evil is forming by every act of obedience or of disobedience to God's law, and the future condition of every human being depends on his real character. There is every grade of character, from the lowest to the highest, and so there will be every grade of future condition. For the Scriptures assure us, that "every man shall receive according to his works, whether they have been good or whether they have been evil." "Whatsoever a man soweth, that also shall he reap." There is no intimation that a good act of a bad man will any more fail of its reward, than a bad act of a good man will miss of its punishment.

There is no such hair-splitting about motives in the Bible as has been introduced by modern theologians. There is no such definition of goodness as that it consists of actions done for the glory of God. The glory of God is too distant and abstruse a motive for the common mass of people to act from. God has given them a much plainer rule of conduct, whether an action be wrong or right. Christ has concentrated the whole of social, religious duty in one formula, which appeals solely to man's natural sense of justice: — "Whatsoever ye would that men should do to you, do ye even so to them; for this is the law and the prophets." This is the sum and essence of religious duty. There is no proviso, that it all must be done for the glory of God.

Man is created to act from a variety of motives. It is very seldom that he acts from one alone. They rise in moral worth, from abject fear up to doing right because it is right, which is the highest motive of all. The moral desert of an action depends on the predominance of one class of motives over another. But it is better for a man to do right from the lowest motive, than to do wrong. Every motive is appealed to in the Bible. "Honor thy father and thy mother," — why? — "that thy days may be long." "The *fear* of the Lord is the ***beginning*** of wisdom." And it is said of our Saviour, that it was for "the joy set before him" that he endured the cross, despising the shame. "Blessed are the pure in heart," — why? — "for they shall see God." "Whatsoever good thing any man doeth, the same shall he receive of the Lord."

Probation for eternity is confined to no class. Every human being, whether he be called saint or sinner, is fixing his future condition by what he is doing every day of his life. Heathen and Christian are all on trial, and preparing for reward or punishment. "God will render to every man according to his deeds; to them who, by patient continuance in well-doing, seek for glory, and honor, and immortality, eternal life; but unto them that are contentious, and obey not the truth, but obey unrighteousness, indignation and wrath; tribulation and anguish upon every soul of man that doeth evil, of the Jew first, *and also of the Gentile:* but glory, honor, and peace to every man that worketh good; to the Jew first, and also *to the Gentile:* for there is no respect of persons with God."

There is no distinction here made between morality and religion. "Glory, honor, and peace to every man that worketh good, to the Jew first, and also to the Gentile," must include all mankind, in all their actions, and "good" is that which is pronounced to be good by the law written on the heart. "They that have done good shall come forth to the resurrection of life, and they that have done evil to the resurrection of condemnation."

An outward compliance with a mere ritual religion may become the most dangerous snare to which a man can be exposed. The observances of a ceremonial religion may have the effect to lull conscience to sleep, as well as to arouse it to action and vigilance; and the most gigantic vices of heart and life may grow up under the very altars of God. Christ quite as often denounced the religionists of his day as he did the careless and profane. "Woe unto you, Scribes and Pharisees, hypocrites! for ye devour widows' houses, and for a pretence make long prayer: therefore ye shall receive the greater damnation. Woe unto you, Scribes and Pharisees, hypocrites! for ye compass sea and land to make one proselyte, and when he is made, ye make him twofold more the child of hell than yourselves." "Woe unto you, Scribes and Pharisees, hypocrites! for ye are like whited sepulchres, which indeed appear beautiful outward, but are within full of dead men's bones, and of all uncleanness." They persecuted Christ for breaking the Sabbath by healing on that day, and so great was their self-deception that they did it with murder in their hearts. He who knew men's hearts carried it home to their consciences: — "Is it lawful to do good on the Sabbath days, or to do evil; to save life, or to destroy it?"

The most awful crimes that have ever been committed have been perpetrated under cover of religion. Thus it was that Naboth was robbed of his vineyard and his life by Jezebel, the wife of Ahab. "I," said she to her husband, "will give thee the vineyard of Naboth the Jezreelite. So she wrote letters in Ahab's name, and sealed them with his seal, and sent the letters unto the elders and the nobles that were in his city, dwelling with Naboth. And she wrote in the letters, saying, *Proclaim a fast*, and set Naboth on high among the people ; and set two men, sons of Belial, before him, to bear witness against him, saying, thou didst blaspheme God and the king. And then carry him out and stone him, that he may die " ! This was to be done at a public fast, that no suspicion might be fixed on those who were the instigators of it !

Religion has in all ages been liable to be separated from morality, and thus made to degenerate into a dead form, petrifying instead of softening the heart. It was so in the days of Isaiah. He was sent to the Israelites with such a message as this : — " To what purpose is the multitude of your sacrifices unto me ? saith the Lord. I am full of the burnt-offerings of rams, and the fat of fed beasts ; and I delight not in the blood of bullocks, or of lambs, or of he-goats. When ye come to appear before me, who hath required this at your hand to tread my courts ? Bring no more vain oblations : incense is an abomination unto me ; the new moons and Sabbaths, the calling of assemblies, I cannot away with ; it is iniquity, even the solemn meeting. Your new moons and your appointed feasts my soul hateth : they are a trouble unto me ; I am weary to bear them. And when ye spread forth your hands, I will hide mine eyes from you ; yea, when ye make many prayers I will not hear : your hands are full of blood. *Wash ye, make you clean ;* put away the evil of your doings from before mine eyes ; cease to do evil ; learn to do well ; seek judgment, relieve the oppressed, judge the fatherless, plead for the widow." The Scriptures are full of such representations. "He that hath my commandments," saith the Saviour, "and keepeth them, he it is that loveth me ; and he that loveth me shall be loved of my Father."

These are the doctrines we preach, and if we are condemned for preaching mere morality, the Scriptures themselves must come under the same censure. No man ever heard, in this pulpit, at least, morality separated from religion. No man ever heard morality commended upon the worldly maxim, that honesty is the best policy. We preach religious faith, religious emotion, religious experience, and morality, when based upon these principles, is itself religion.

We admit that we place integrity at the foundation of character, moral and religious. Without it, all pretensions to religion become as sounding brass and a tinkling cymbal. We admit that we are especially careful to examine the moral character of those who make the greatest religious professions, and are most given to turning the world upside down to make converts to godliness.

And may the worst reproach ever brought against us be, that we are distinguished among mankind for the strictest moral integrity. We profess to cultivate the most spiritual religion, but the only announcement that we care to make of it to the world is by the fruit of a Christian life.

DISCOURSE V.

UNITARIANISM EVANGELICAL CHRISTIANITY.

FOR WHILE ONE SAITH, I AM OF PAUL, AND ANOTHER, I AM OF APOLLOS, ARE YE NOT CARNAL? — 1 Corinthians iii. 4.

I AM this evening to speak to you of the epithet *Evangelical*, as arrogated by certain classes of Christians, and denied to others. I wish to ascertain its import, and the propriety of its application to some, and its denial to others, who claim the Christian name. It is intended to intimate the idea of a special purity of doctrine and sanctity of life as belonging to those who claim it. Its denial is intended to cast a reproach on those from whom it is withheld, of laxity of doctrine, and a life less scrupulously exact.

It will be the purpose of this discourse to inquire, first, What are the pretensions of the Evangelical Christians? In the second place, Have these pretensions any good foundation? And, thirdly, Who are justly entitled to the name of Evangelical Christians?

As it happens, we have the means at hand of ascertaining what are the pretensions of those who arrogate to themselves the title of Evangelical Christians. Nearly two years ago, a "World's Convention" was held in London, by those who supposed themselves to be especially entitled to this appellation, in order to form what they denominated an "Evangelical Alliance."

After a session of a fortnight, they published the result of their deliberations in the following resolutions and articles of faith: —

"Resolved, That this conference, composed of professing Christians of many differing denominations, all exercising the right of private judgment, and, through common infirmity, differing among themselves in the views they entertain on some points, both of Christian doctrine and ecclesiastical polity, and gathered together from many and remote parts of the earth, for the purpose of promoting Christian union, rejoice in making the avowal of the glorious truth, that the Church of the living God, while it admits of growth, is one church, never having lost, and being incapable of losing, its essential unity. Not, therefore, to create that unity, but to confess it, is their design in assembling together. One in reality, they desire, also, as far as they may be able to attain it, to be visibly one, and thus both to realize in themselves, and to exhibit to others, that a living and everlasting union binds all true believers together in the fellowship of the Church of Christ, 'which is his body, the fulness of him that filleth all in all.'

"That this conference, while recognizing the essential unity of the Christian Church, feel constrained to deplore its existing divisions, and to express their deep sense of the sinfulness involved in the alienation of affection by which they have been attended, and of the manifold evils which have resulted therefrom, and to avow their solemn conviction of the necessity and duty of taking measures, in humble dependence on the Divine blessing, towards attaining a state of mind and feeling more in accordance with the word and spirit of Christ Jesus.

"That therefore the members of this conference are deeply convinced of the desirableness of forming a confederation on the basis of great Evangelical principles held in common by them, which may afford opportunity to members of the Church of Christ of cultivating brotherly love, enjoying Christian intercourse, and promoting such other objects as they may hereafter agree to prosecute together; and they hereby proceed to form such a confederation, under the name of 'the Evangelical Alliance.'

"That with a view, however, of furnishing the most satisfactory explanation, and guarding against misconception in regard to their design and the means of its attainment, they deem it expedient explicitly to state as follows.

"That the parties composing the Alliance shall be such persons only as hold and maintain what are usually understood to be Evangelical views in regard to the matters of doctrine understated, viz.: —

"1. The Divine inspiration, authority, and sufficiency of the Holy Scriptures.

"2. The unity of the Godhead, and the trinity of persons therein.

"3. The utter depravity of human nature, in consequence of the fall.

"4. The incarnation of the Son of God, his work of atonement for the sins of mankind, and his mediatorial intercession and reign.

"5. The justification of the sinner by faith alone.

"6. The work of the Holy Spirit, in the conversion and sanctification of the sinner.

"7. The right and duty of private judgment in the interpretation of the Holy Scriptures.

"8. The Divine institution of the Christian ministry, and the authority and perpetuity of the ordinances of baptism and the Lord's Supper.

"9. The immortality of the soul, the resurrection of the body, the judgment of the world by the Lord Jesus Christ, with the eternal blessedness of the righteous, and the eternal punishment of the wicked."

Such are the principles and such are the claims of those who denominate themselves Evangelical, or Gospel Christians, for Evangelical is the Greek word for Gospel.

Let us now analyze these claims and principles, and see to what they amount.

In the first place, it appears that the term "Evangelical" is sectarian and exclusive, for the parties composing the Alliance declare that it shall be of such persons *only* as hold and maintain what are usually understood to be Evangelical views in regard to certain doctrines. Yet they profess to be *the true church*, and the *only* true church. "They rejoice in making their unanimous avowal of the glorious truth, that the Church of the living God is *one* church. "One in reality, they desire, also, as far as they may be able to attain it, *to be* visibly one, and thus both to *realize in themselves*, and to *exhibit* to others, that a living and everlasting union binds *all true believers* together in the fellowship of the Church of Christ."

The meaning of this cannot be mistaken. They wish to realize in themselves, and to exhibit to others, that a living and everlasting union binds *all true believers* together in the fellowship of the Church of Christ.

Yet they acknowledge that they differ among themselves, and belong to different denominations, for the first resolution runs in this way : — "Resolved, that this conference, composed of professing Christians, of *different* denominations, all exercising the right of private judgment, and, through common infirmity, *differing* among themselves in the views they severally entertain *on some points* of doctrine and polity," &c.

What, then, was the sum and substance of what was done by the World's Convention ? The representatives of several small fragments of the Church Universal, amounting in all to perhaps one sixteenth of the whole, meet together and resolve that the Church of the living God is *one*, and that *they are* that one true church ; that the differences of opinion among themselves are unimportant, and may be overlooked, while the differences between themselves and the rest of the so-called Christian world are fundamental, and shut out all else from the fold of the true believers.

They profess to be Protestants, and lay down as the fundamental principles of their association the two points on which their ancestors separated from the Church of Rome, — "The sufficiency of the Scriptures, and the right of private judgment." But they draw up nine articles of alliance, which are intended to shut out from their body for ever all those, who, in the *exercise* of their private judgment, arrive at different conclusions from themselves, and which are intended to bind themselves and their successors just as much as the creed of Nice or Constantinople, or the canons of the Council of Trent.

They came together to promote the *union* of the Christian Church, but pass nine articles of faith which unchurch and excommunicate fifteen sixteenths, or perhaps nineteen twentieths, of the Christian world. All the Roman Catholic Church is amputated at a blow. All the Greek Church is put at once without the pale. The article on the utter depravity of hu-

man nature closes the door on the Arminian portion of the Episcopal Church in England, and the liberal portion of the Dissenters. It disowns a large division of every Orthodox church throughout the world. The article on the Trinity cuts off all the Unitarians of the continent of Europe, a large and increasing body, all the Unitarians in the kingdom of Great Britain, and in the United States. The article upon the eternity of the punishment of the wicked excludes all the Universalists of Germany, (for even the most orthodox there, on other points, are heretical on this,) and all embracing the same tenets in the United States.

Narrowed down by such huge subtractions, the Evangelical Alliance becomes one of the most insignificant, as well as most arrogant, bodies that ever assembled on earth. They do nothing but declare themselves the only true church, and then adjourn, and return home just as much separated and divided as ever, and resume their old attitude of mutual repulsion and antagonism, and call themselves after the names of Paul, Apollos, and Cephas, just as much as ever.

When we analyze the articles of confederation, we find that *Evangelical* is nothing more nor less than *Orthodox* under a new name, meaning by Orthodoxy that which has been such since the Reformation, which is Calvinism and Trinitarianism, the doctrines of the tri-personality of God, the total corruption of human nature, and regeneration by exclusive Divine agency.

We now come to the second part of our inquiry, the *propriety* of the assumption of the title of Evangelical by those who framed the nine articles of confederation. Evangelical, we have already said, means Gospel. Gospel is taken for the Christian religion, or it may mean the teachings of Christ recorded by the Evangelists in the four Gospels, contrasted with the Epistles and the rest of the New Testament.

If we take Evangelical in the first sense, as meaning the whole New Testament, the New Testament is *not* the basis of the alliance, it is the nine articles, which are a sectarian interpretation of the New Testament. Not one half of the Christian Church, since the beginning, have believed that the Son was equal to the Father; and original sin and justification by faith alone have met with a very partial reception, even in those churches which have incorporated them into their creeds. The "Evangelical Alliance," then, is *not* the proper title of an association which does not found their union upon the simple New Testament without note or comment. It is *not* Evangelical, it is sectarian.

Had the Alliance confined itself to the first and seventh articles of their confederation, they would have been truly Evangelical in their principles. They are, "the Divine inspiration, authority, and sufficiency of the Holy Scriptures," and "the right and duty of private judgment in the interpretation of the Scriptures." They would, in that case, have stood upon the broad basis of the whole New Testament, the whole and entire Gospel, as it addresses itself to every human mind.

There is another and an important sense of the word Evangelical, or Gospel, as signifying the teachings of Christ as recorded in the four Evangelists, in distinction from the rest of the New Testament. This distinction is broad and essential. The teachings of Christ stand apart and far above the rest of the New Testament. To him the spirit was given not by measure. In his word, the *whole* system of the Gospel was complete and perfect from the first hour of his teaching. His last discourse to his disciples was followed by a prayer, in which he says, — "I have *finished* the work which thou gavest me to do. I have given them the words which thou gavest me." Speaking of himself as the Messiah, he says, — "Thou hast given him power over all flesh, that he should give eternal life to as many as thou hast given him. And this is life eternal, that they might know thee the only true God, and Jesus Christ whom thou hast sent." That knowledge he speaks of himself as *having imparted* to his disciples. They were qualified to be his apostles by the fact of having been the eye and ear witnesses of what he had done and what he had taught. The Holy

Spirit was promised them that they might "bring to remembrance" what he had taught them. Future revelations were not to make known any new doctrines, but merely to explain what Christ himself had taught. "He shall take of mine and show it unto you." The Apostles were likewise to receive, by Divine communication, knowledge of future events. "He shall show you things to come." After his resurrection, he commissioned his disciples, — "Go and teach all nations," "teaching them to observe *whatsoever I have commanded you.*" The disciples, during his ministry, had a very imperfect comprehension of his religion, and light dawned very gradually upon their minds. It was nearly ten years before they understood the extent of their commission, that they were commanded to preach the Gospel literally to all nations.

The Gospels contain Christianity just as Christ preached it, expressed in general principles and propositions, addressed to universal humanity. The Epistles are the same truths adapted to particular persons and circumstances, and are enforced by illustrations and modes of argument which were adapted to individuals and classes, to meet their prejudices and conform to their modes of speech. It is difficult to distinguish, often, which is the truth and which is the illustration. So much is this the case, that Peter, in one of his Epistles, speaks of the writings of Paul as obscure and difficult to be understood, and liable to be wrested from their true meaning. Such writings, surely, ought not to be put on a level with the Gospels.

Paul confessed that he and his fellow-Apostles "knew but in part, and prophesied but in part." The knowledge of Christ was *perfect.* "I am the Way, and the Truth, and the Life ; no man cometh unto the Father but by me." "The law was given by Moses, but grace and truth came by Jesus Christ." In him, the word or revelation of God became incarnate. "The word was made flesh and dwelt among us." "No man hath seen God at any time ; the only begotten Son, who is in the bosom of the Father, he hath declared him." Paul sometimes gave his own personal advice, without pretending to any Divine illumination.

For these reasons the Gospels ought to be distinguished from the Epistles, and placed far above them. One is the text, and the other the commentary. One is the constitution, and the other the history of its administration. One is the fountain-head, the other the streams which flow from it, with various admixtures.

Now how do the Evangelical doctrines, as they are called, stand related to the Gospels and Epistles? Calvin, the great expositor of the Evangelical system in modern times, while he was a minister in Geneva, preached over a thousand public discourses. How many, think you, were preached from a text in the

Gospels ? Not one in a hundred, and the greater part from the Epistles. Take up the Westminster Confession, and examine the proof-texts of the article on justification by faith, and you will find that forty-two out of forty-three are from other parts of the Bible, and only one from the Gospels. Can this be considered an Evangelical or Gospel doctrine, when there is nothing, with the exception of a single text, to found it on in the Gospels ?

Turn to the article on original sin, and you will find eighty-five quotations from the Scriptures to sustain it. Out of the eighty-five, only two are from the Gospels. Is this to be considered an Evangelical or Gospel doctrine, when only two out of eighty-five texts, which are imagined to sustain it, are found in the Gospels, and most of them are from the writings of Paul ? Is not this putting the disciple above his master ? Is not this saying "I am of Paul," rather than "I am of Christ" ? Can that be said to be Evangelical doctrine, which finds little or no support from the Evangelists ? Can that be said to be Christian doctrine, concerning which Christ taught nothing ?

It is difficult to conceive of a name more inappropriate than *Evangelical*, as applied, first, to a class of Christians who make, not the New Testament, but their sectarian deductions from the New Testament, the basis of their association ; and, in the second place, who take their leading doctrines, not from the Gospels, the writings of the four Evangelists, the teachings of Jesus, but from the writings of Paul.

Let us now consider whom they exclude as unworthy of the name Evangelical.

In the first place, they exclude, particularly and pointedly, all Unitarians. Let us examine the justice of this.

Unitarians take the Bible, particularly the New Testament, as their *only* creed. They take the whole Gospel as the basis of their association. They do not extract from it any peculiar sectarian interpretation, and lay it down as a condition of communion with them, and of the extension to others of the Christian name and privileges. They religiously abstain from any such act as the formation of a written creed. Christ and his Apostles never did any such thing. Had it been necessary to the welfare of the Christian Church to have a creed, they would have instituted one. The effect of creeds from the beginning has been, not to unite, but to divide, the Christian Church ; not to produce harmony, but dissension. It is always an attempt of the majority to coerce the minority, and is felt by that minority to be an enormous oppression, and thus occasions, not only dispute, but alienation of feeling, which is more antichristian than any mere diversity of opinion. Christ has commanded us to " call no man master, for one is your Master, even Christ, and all ye are brethren." It is an act of disrespect to Christ to interpose between him and those whom he came to instruct, by attempting to dictate to them the sense in which they shall receive his instructions. There will always be great diversities of opinion among men on the plainest subjects. You can never find two persons who give the same account of a discourse to which they have just listened. You cannot find two Christians, of the most eminent piety and intelligence, who will agree in their opinions on the most common points of Christian doctrine. Subscription to the same articles does not create a uniformity of belief. If it does not, it expresses what does not exist, it is insincere, it operates to disparage and exclude the honest, and to give power to the unscrupulous and ambitious.

Another reason why we abstain from making a creed is the fact, that religious knowledge is progressive. The Gospel continues the same, but our understanding of it may be improved. There is no propriety in declaring beforehand, at the very commencement of our studies, to what conclusions we shall come. It is equally absurd for one age to attempt to dictate the religious opinions of the next.

For these reasons, the Unitarians as a body have religiously abstained from forming a creed. We associate upon the basis of the Gospel alone, without note or comment. We insist upon, and carry out to the letter, " the sufficiency of the Scriptures and the right of private judgment." We claim, therefore, that the distinction Evangelical, or Gospel, Christians belongs preëminently to us.

We contend, that, in forbearing to write a creed, we are the true and consistent advocates of union. All creeds are, in their own nature, sectarian and disorganizing. They are, in the first place, the fruit of sectarianism, and then they reproduce sectarianism without limit and without end.

Finally, we claim to be Gospel or Evangelical Christians, because we go to the Gospels, and to the Gospels alone, for our religion. Christ is our only Master, our only infallible Teacher. No doctrine is received by us, which is not clearly taught in the four Evangelists. Christ taught the *whole* of his own religion, in its true form and relative proportions. The Acts and the Epistles contain the history of its administration by the Apostles, for the first thirty years. It received a coloring from the personal peculiarities of each, and was shaped to suit the circumstances, to meet the prejudices, of different communities. Much of the Epistles is taken up in discussing questions which were of a local and temporary character, and which lost their interest and their application in after ages, when the circumstances of the churches changed. Not so the Gospels. They are addressed to man as man, to man in the nineteenth century as well as in the first. The Epistle to the Hebrews is addressed to the Jews, or rather to the converts to Christianity from among the ancient people of God, and is filled with arguments and modes of illustration, which might be striking and conclusive to them, but not so to a person who had not had a Jewish education. The Epistle to the Romans is an attempt to reconcile the discordant elements of the Christian Church, made up as it was of converts from Paganism and Judaism, and to show them that they came into the fold of Christ upon a perfect equality. The Epistles to the Corinthians are intended to correct the abuses which had crept into that church in the absence of Paul, and to answer inquiries which the church wished to make of him on some points of doctrine or duty.

The Gospels, on the other hand, which are the teaching of Christ, contain the *abstract essence* of Christianity, and are addressed to universal humanity; not to Jew or Gentile, but to man, — to his moral and religious nature. To them, therefore, we defer, on them we rest our faith, by them we would regulate our conduct, on them we repose our hopes, and therefore *we* claim to be regarded as *preëminently* Evangelical Christians.

There is another pretension put forth by those who style themselves Evangelical Christians, which it is proper that I should here examine. It is, that they are the only depositaries of divine truth. Belonging to the Evangelical body is equivalent to belonging to an infallible church. The chain of reasoning by which this pretension is sustained is something like this. Human nature is essentially depraved, and in its natural state has no discernment of spiritual things, and, of course, has no right to an opinion upon religious subjects. Part of mankind are regenerated, and created anew by the renovating influences of the Holy Spirit. Those who are so regenerated uniformly embrace Evangelical opinions. One of the fruits of the work of the Spirit on the heart is the conviction of our lost and undone condition by nature, of the necessity of an infinite atonement for sin, and, of course, of a trinity of infinite persons to enact the parts required in the scheme of the atonement. This is, perhaps, the shortest and most effectual way to the establishment of an exclusive and infallible church, that has ever been devised.

The Romanists have a similar argument for the exclusive jurisdiction of their church in religious matters. They make a distinction between faith and belief. Belief is the assent which any human mind gives to any proposition, upon the preponderance of evidence in its favor. It is not accompanied by certainty. Faith, on the other hand, is the gift of God, and confers upon him to whom it is given, not only persuasion, but certainty. This faith is an exclusive gift to all true Catholics, and by it they are made to *know* that they are right. What the Catholic Church gains by an exclusive faith, the Evangelical Church secures by an exclusive regeneration. Both arrogate to themselves a monopoly of authority in religious affairs. Where either of them bears sway, they are equally disposed to make the same use of their prerogative, to elevate themselves and put every thing else down. The divine right of having been born again is found just as available for the purpose of spiritual domination, as the divine right of belonging to the only true Apostolic and indivisible church.

You may hear the supreme Deity of Christ established by such an argument as this, drawn from Christian experience. Every converted soul, when brought under the conviction of sin, has felt such a weight of guilt burdening the conscience, that nothing short of an infinite sacrifice could take it away; such a sense of weakness and helplessness, that nothing short of an Almighty Saviour could deliver the sinner. Thus feeling is made the test of truth, and whatever a converted man *feels* to be true, that must be assumed to be fact.

It is made a test of Christian experience, to feel the truth of the Calvinistic dogmas of total depravity and entire inability. He who has never felt these has no pretensions to Christian experience, and, of consequence, his suffrage is not to be taken in matters of faith.

I, for one, protest against all such assumptions, as the worst species of spiritual oppression. There is not a sect in Christendom which may not in the same way establish its claim to be the only true church, and thus excommunicate the rest of the Christian world.

No man was ever more sure than Wesley of his Christian experience, and yet no man was ever more firmly, I might say violently, opposed to Calvinism. He, however, had the good sense and the charity not to make any exclusive claim to piety. The Baptist makes immersion the badge of the true church, and denies that any one not baptized in that way has even the promise of salvation. The Episcopalian founds his claim upon the only true Apostolical succession, and so on through the whole list of Christian sects. It is enough to say, that these conflicting claims mutually destroy each other, and that of the Evangelical Church falls with the rest.

I appeal from all these pretensions to the Bible. I deny that there is any such intellectual test of discipleship to Christ in the Gospel, as assent to the dogmas of Athanasius or Calvin. The test there proposed is a plain one, that of Christian character. "By their fruits ye shall know them." "He that hath my commandments and *keepeth* them, he it is that loveth me, and he that loveth me shall be loved of my Father, and I will love him and manifest myself unto him." To love Christ and keep his commandments has no necessary connection with any system of metaphysics or spiritual philosophy. "The fruit of the spirit is" — what ? belief in certain theological speculations ? — no ; but "love, joy, peace, long-suffering, gentleness, goodness, faith, meekness, temperance." These characteristics of a true discipleship to Christ are not confined to any Christian denomination. They are exhibited in connection with the greatest variety of speculative belief, and, in fact, have very little to do with modes of faith.

The exclusive pretensions of the Evangelical Church cannot be maintained. There is a growing desire throughout Christendom for some better basis of union than has ever yet been proposed. The World's Convention was an abortion, because it was not in accordance with the spirit of the age. That spirit is catholic. The Convention was sectarian. The Church is to be made one, if it ever can be, not upon the basis of the creed of any one sect, but by adhering only to those great and cardinal doctrines which are common to all.

DISCOURSE VI.

UNITARIANISM DOES NOT TEND TO UNBELIEF.

AND IF CHRIST BE NOT RISEN, THEN IS OUR PREACHING VAIN, AND YOUR FAITH IS ALSO VAIN. — 1 Corinthians xv. 14.

THE subject upon which I am to address you this evening is *the alleged tendency of Unitarianism to unbelief.* Those who make this allegation mean by it, that a Unitarian is more liable to abandon all belief in a miraculous revelation than a Trinitarian, and that a community in which Unitarianism is the prevailing faith is more likely to become infidel than a community in which the doctrine of the Trinity is received. This question, which is really an interesting one, I mean to meet with fairness and to discuss with candor.

In the first place I remark, that there are two classes of people who must be thrown out of consideration in discussing this subject, — those who never examine, whose faith is merely traditionary, and those who have abandoned religious faith from moral obliquity. A person who is a Unitarian or a Trinitarian merely because his father and mother were so before him, or because it was taught him in his catechism, is a Unitarian or a Trinitarian merely by accident. His suffrage is not to be taken on any side, as proving the truth or the untruth of any thing. His own mind has not been exercised upon the evidence. His belief, not being founded on evidence, neither strengthens nor weakens any cause, or makes any dogma more or less likely to be true.

So the unbelief of a man, who has been made so by moral causes, is not to be taken into account. Belief is often given up to reconcile the convictions of the mind to the tenor of the life. In Christianity there are the most tremendous moral sanctions. It denounces "the wrath of God against all ungodliness and unrighteousness of men." It predicts the most appalling consequences as the inevitable result of every deviation from the law of rectitude written upon every heart. If Christianity be true, then a wicked life is the worst kind of suicide. It is nothing more nor less than plunging, coolly and deliberately, soul and body into hell. No rational being can feel comfortably under such a state of things, and the only way in which a wicked man can free himself for a moment from a perpetual and haunting consciousness of inevitable perdition is to call in question the truth of Christianity. His objection is not to any particular form of Christianity, but he wants to get rid of it altogether. He catches at any argument, however flimsy, which seems to undermine the solidity of its foundations, and to loosen in any degree the obligations and responsibilities which its truth imposes. This class of persons I place wholly out of view in the present discussion. I speak only of those who are honestly seeking for truth, and whose daily life is such as to make it as much for their interest that Christianity should be true as false.

The question, then, which we are to discuss is, whether Christianity, to an inquiring mind, is as credible when it is considered as teaching the peculiar doctrines of Calvinism and Trinitarianism, as it is without them, and considered as teaching merely those doctrines which Unitarians find in it.

It is usual for the opponents of Unitarianism to appeal to experience. And, appealing to experience, they say, and it has passed into a proverb, that "Unitarianism is the half-way house to infidelity." Once begin to doubt the Trinity and the doctrines of grace, as they are called, and there is no knowing when you will stop. Unitarianism will not long afford a resting-place. You will doubt on, and give up one thing after another, till you land in total unbelief. The history of individuals is pointed out as exemplifying this. Germany is spoken of as a demonstration of this fact. So convinced are some portions of the Christian Church of the saving power of Trinitarianism and Calvinism over a belief in the Bible, that they advocate the maintenance and enforcement of a written creed, in which these doctrines are incorporated, in order to sustain and preserve a belief in the Bible itself. Without written creeds, it is declared to be impossible to keep churches, first, out of Unitarianism, and, finally, out of total unbelief.

I deny that there is any such power in a Trinitarian and Calvinistic creed to keep unbelief out of the world. The Athanasian creed certainly did not keep unbelief out of France during the last century and the present. Nor does it out of Italy. The three creeds of the Episcopal Church have not kept unbelief out of England, nor do the most orthodox creeds in this country succeed in preventing hundreds and thousands from feeling a total distrust towards the whole of Christianity, under the very pulpits whence Trinitarianism and Calvinism are fulminated every Sunday.

But there is more expressed than is intended in the saying, that Unitarianism is the half-way house to infidelity. The very phraseology shows, that, from the circumstances of the case, Unitarianism has not a fair chance to afford rest to him who entertains it under such conditions. He is in a transition state from believing too much to believing too little. He has acquired too much momentum, in his descent from the bleak and barren regions of dogmatism towards the dark and misty fens of unbelief, to stop in the temperate, vital, and genial region of truth, which is equally removed from both extremes. Those whose moral natures revolt from the awful injustice of the Calvinistic system, and refuse to clothe the Deity in the gloomy horrors of that faith, — those whose intellects cannot receive the dogma of the Trinity, which confounds at once arithmetic and mental individuality, — have generally contracted a prejudice against the Bible itself, with which, in their minds, these doctrines have been identified. It requires time and labor to disentangle these associated ideas, and to free the Scriptures from the suspicion of extravagance and contradiction, which the detection of great mistakes first casts over them. There are multitudes who have reason to thank God that there is such a blessed half-way house as Unitarianism between dogmatism and unbelief; for in it they have found rest to their souls, light to their understandings, a firm foundation to their faith, comfort in life, and hope in death.

But this very saying, that Unitarianism is the half-way house to infidelity, though intended as a reproach against Unitarianism, to my mind contains an admission in its favor. Its very structure shows that doubt is not supposed to *commence* when the subject of it is in Unitarianism, but in a state of Orthodoxy. It is *no* half-way house to one who has never been Orthodox. It does not assert, what would not be true, that doubt *originates* in the state of Unitarianism. It is supposed to originate when Christianity is identified with Calvinism and Trinitarianism. And this I believe to be the case. The most cultivated minds in all Orthodox churches listen with incredulity, or a very qualified assent, to the dogmas of the Trinity, incarnation, the fall, vicarious punishment, &c., &c. The famous John Foster, of England, long ago wrote a treatise to account for the aversion of men of taste to Evangelical religion. He might have cut the matter short by saying, that the peculiar dogmas of Evangelical religion are inconsistent, unreasonable, and contradictory to the first principles of morality and justice, and therefore in themselves improbable; and, as such, are most likely to be seen to be so by the most enlightened and cultivated minds. They are *confessed* to be unreasonable, and their credit is saved by saying that they are *above* reason, or mysteries, and, therefore, that reason has no right to decide against them.

But let us analyze this matter, and see if there be no greater objections against Christianity, when considered as teaching Orthodoxy, than when teaching simple Unitarianism.

What are the objections which are usually brought against the credibility of a miraculous revelation? In the first place, it is objected to revelation that it is not *universal*. If it is necessary to man's spiritual welfare, a good and impartial God would have imparted it to all mankind, and not have withheld it from any. If it is not necessary, then he would not have given it to any. This *is* the strongest objection to the antecedent probability of a revelation. I do not say that it is unanswerable, for I believe that it admits of an answer. But it lies with equal force against Trinitarianism and Unitarianism.

The second grand objection to the credibility of a revelation is *to the credibility of miracles*, by which alone revelation can be given and authenticated. Hume tells us, that miracles are in themselves incredible, and incapable of being authenticated, and therefore, instead of authenticating a revelation to which they are appended, they make it less credible than it would be without them. This argument has given the defenders of revelation much trouble. That it may be satisfactorily answered I have no doubt, or I should not continue to preach a religion which I did not believe. Paul, in our text, stakes the truth of Christianity on a miracle, on the resurrection of Christ. "If Christ be *not* risen, then is our preaching vain, and your faith is also vain." If miracles under *all* circumstances are incredible, then is Christianity incredible, for it is founded on miracle. But the objection is equally strong against the credibility of a revelation, when it is thought to teach Trinitarianism or Unitarianism.

But what purports to be a revelation may be more or less credible, on account of what it contains. It may be consistent in its parts, and it may be inconsistent. It may contain representations of God which are agreeable to what we know of him by the light of nature, or it may contain representations which are repugnant to them. The unity of God, for instance, is a probable doctrine, considered as a doctrine of revelation, because it agrees with all the phenomena of the universe ; for the whole universe bears the marks of being the work of *one* mind, of *one only* designing and superintending cause. There is an internal probability in the first verse of the Old Testament, — "In the beginning, God created the heavens and the earth." The human mind assents to it, as not only sublime, but true. It corresponds with the intuitions of reason. Such an expression is worthy of a Divine revelation, especially when we consider it as addressed to a world of idolaters, who worshipped the various *parts* of the visible universe as God.

So, when we turn to the New Testament, and read the first verse of John's Gospel, — "In the beginning was the Word, and the Word was with God, and the Word was God," — if we interpret the phrase "Word" to mean an *attribute* of God, that God made the world by his power and wisdom, figuratively represented as his word, we have a mere repetition, in other language, of the assertion of the first chapter of Genesis.

But if we interpret the "Word" to mean a person, the second person of a trinity, then we introduce confusion and improbability into the very subject-matter of revelation itself. There is *no* antecedent probability, that God should exist in a trinity. There is no intimation of such a mode of existence in reason or nature. And if there were persons in God, there is no reason, or intimation in nature or reason, that those persons should be three, rather than four or five. It is antecedently improbable that one equal person of a trinity should use the agency of another equal person of the trinity in creating the world. But those who maintain the doctrine of the Trinity assert that it was *through* the Son that the Father created the world. Such a doctrine is essentially *improbable*, and would make the theology of the New Testament, not an improvement upon that of the Old, but a corruption of it.

Then the relations of the persons of the Trinity to each other, that of Father and Son, and the Holy Ghost as proceeding from them both, makes the Trinity of the New Testament much more like the mythology of the heathen than the pure spirituality and sublime simplicity of the Jehovah of the Old Testament.

It is true, that, to my mind, and those of all Unitarians, the New Testament teaches no such doctrine, but teaches the same unity and spirituality of the Deity which pervade the Old Testament. But did it contain such a doctrine as the Trinity, it would require a much larger amount and stronger degree of external evidence to authenticate such a revelation as coming from God, than if it conformed to the simple doctrine of Moses and the prophets.

Let us next contrast the doctrines of *inspiration*

and *incarnation* as to their essential probability. The doctrine of the Trinity involves the doctrine of incarnation. And what *is* the doctrine of incar nation ? It is, that the second person of the Trin ity, the Son, very and eternal God, a being inhabiting immensity and eternity, descended to the earth and became incarnate in the body of an unborn infant, and together with the human soul of that infant made one person, never to be again divided, and that that union for ever subsists. Omnipotence and human weakness coalesced. Omniscience was united to the mind of a child, who *grew in wisdom* and in stature, and in favor with God and man. And some have carried the idea of incarnation so far as to say, that the second person of the Trinity died upon the cross, and all affirm that the connection of the Deity with the soul of Christ rendered his sufferings in the hour of crucifixion of infinite merit to atone for the sins of the world. I venture to affirm, that there is not an invention in all heathen mythology which carries with it stronger internal marks of improbability than this. It will not bear examination for a moment. It contradicts all the most essential Divine attributes. The immutable God *changed* his mode of existence, and lived thirty-three years upon earth, and then reascended to heaven. God, who is incapable of suffering, permitted himself to be taken, condemned, and crucified, by his own creatures. Reverence is as much shocked as reason by these propositions.

Would not a revelation which contained such propositions require a much greater amount of external evidence to make it credible, than one which maintained unimpaired the integrity of the Divine perfections, not to say the dignity of the Divine character?

The Unitarian believes, as much as the Trinitarian, all that is related concerning Jesus of Nazareth in the New Testament, and as much believes in him as the Saviour of the world. But he believes that every thing that he was and accomplished may be as well accounted for on the supposition of his *inspiration*, that God clothed him with his power and filled him with his wisdom, as that the second person of a trinity became incarnate in him. He believes that that Scripture was literally fulfilled in him which he quoted in the synagogue of Nazareth, and applied to himself, — "The spirit of the Lord is upon me, because he hath *anointed* me to preach the Gospel to the poor; he hath sent me to heal the broken-hearted. . . . . . This day is this Scripture fulfilled in your ears." And what Peter said of him in his speech to Cornelius, — "How God *anointed* Jesus of Nazareth with the Holy Ghost and with power, who went about doing good, and healing all that were oppressed of the Devil, for *God was with him*." Or, as he said of himself, — "The words that I speak unto you, I speak not of myself; the *Father* that dwelleth in me, *he* doeth the works." Inspiration, the communication of supernatural power and knowledge to Christ, carries with it no internal marks of extravagance and improbability. It is analogous to the power and knowledge which God gives to every man by the natural exercise of his faculties. The enlightenment and spiritual salvation of mankind through Jesus of Nazareth is analogous to the way in which God has advanced the human race in science, learning, and civilization, through intellects of great wisdom and power, which he has raised up, apparently, for this especial purpose.

But the incarnation of God, the amalgamation of an Infinite Spirit with a finite soul into one person, the birth, the human life, the death, burial, resurrection, and ascension of God, are ideas which are self-contradictory, and give the impress of extravagance to any system of theology of which they make a part. They require, therefore, a greater amount of external evidence to prove them to come from God, than the doctrine of the inspiration of Jesus.

The same thing holds true of the doctrine of the fall. That the essential constitution of human nature was changed by one transgression of our first parents, so that their offspring come into the world incapable of any good, and capable only of evil, is essentially incredible. It would give that sin a nature wholly different from any other sin that ever was committed. No other sin that ever was committed had the same power to change human nature. It is *essentially im-*

probable that this sin had any such power. It could only be by an arbitrary and extraordinary appointment of God. No reason can be given why he should have made such an arbitrary and extraordinary appointment. Not only is it improbable on that account, but it is wholly subversive of God's moral attributes. It would have been an act of injustice, in comparison to which all the injustice that has ever been perpetrated by men in this world would be as a drop of water to the ocean, as the small dust of the balance to the mighty bulk of the globe itself. That myriads on myriads of the human race should be cast into eternal torment for a sin of which they were not only innocent, but absolutely ignorant, is a doctrine more improbable, I had almost said, than atheism itself, and strips the Deity of all the attributes which make him the object of religious regard and affection.

If we interpret the Oriental apologue of the enticing serpent and the forbidden fruit, of the manner in which moral evil first came into the world, and always comes into the world, — as the result of human freedom and frailty surrounded with temptation, — then it conveys a great moral truth, which is consistent with the equity of the Divine government, and holds a proper place in the introduction to the moral and religious history of our race.

Just so it is with the doctrine of *vicarious punishment.* The dogma, that Christ, during the agony of his crucifixion, suffered the punishment that was merited by the sins of the whole human race, or even the elect, carries with it the essential features of extravagance and improbability. That, without such suffering endured by him, God never could have forgiven the penitent, limits the power of the Omnipotent, and gives the idea of helpless imbecility and unskilfulness to the Perfect Ruler of the universe. But that he should have suffered death in consequence of his preaching a Gospel of humility, holiness, and self-denial, to a proud, worldly, and sensual generation, is perfectly credible, and that God should have overruled his death to the establishment of his religion and the demonstration of the immortality of the soul. It is perfectly analogous to other arrangements by which he brings good out of evil.

How can it possibly be said, then, with any pretension to fairness, that the adoption of Unitarian principles tends to unbelief, when every article of faith which Unitarianism discards is in itself unreasonable, incredible, and therefore improbable ? How can it be said, that Unitarianism tends to unbelief, when its articles of faith are in themselves more reasonable and more analogous to the course of nature and the acknowledged principles of the Divine government, than the system to which they are opposed ? I know of no principle upon which this can be affirmed, unless it be this, — that the shortest way to belief is to adopt some article of faith into the creed by which reason is wholly prostrated, confounded, and silenced, and then any thing may be admitted into the mind without question or examination.

I *deny* that there are more skeptics under Unitarian than Orthodox preaching. On the contrary, I affirm that the most frequent cause of unbelief, the great reason why the lofty teaching of the Saviour is rejected, or listened to with apathy and indifference in Christian congregations, is the unreasonable, unjust, and contradictory doctrines which are interpolated into Christianity, and are made to supersede and hide from view the sublime and rational teaching of Christ's Sermon on the Mount.

The human mind does *not* revolt at the fact as incredible, that God has made a revelation to man, but it *does* listen with incredulity to doctrines, as coming from revelation, which are inconsistent with themselves, and wholly irreconcilable with what God has already taught us through nature and reason, consciousness and experience. It is *not* the simple fact, that God has sent Jesus to be the Light of the world, the Ambassador of his mercy, the Pattern of a perfect life, the Vanquisher of death, and the Pledge of immortality to man, that fills the mind with perplexity and the heart with distrust. It is the doctrine of the *Trinity*, confounding at once arithmetic and reason; the doctrine of *incarnation*, by which the wildest fancies of heathen mythology are surpassed; the doctrine of the *fall*, which covers the Divine administration with the ignominy of defeat at its very inception; the doctrine of ***human inability***, by which the sense of accountability, the very key-stone of the arch of religion, is taken out; the doctrine of ***arbitrary and unconditional election***, and ***eternal torments*** for the sin of Adam, — these are the doctrines that spread the paralysis of unbelief over the world, and neutralize the benign influence of the blessed Gospel of Jesus Christ.

It may be objected to all this, I am aware, by the opponent of Unitarianism, that it is mere speculation. Facts are altogether on the other side. Germany is often quoted as an instance of a whole people declining, first into Unitarianism, and then into total unbelief. Unitarian clergymen have given up belief in Christianity, and finally abandoned their profession, in this country. I answer, that not a greater number of Unitarian clergymen have forsaken their calling than of those of other modes of faith. It is greatly to be feared, that unbelief is not confined to the clergy of any denomination, as nothing but unbelief can explain the awful depravity and the appalling crimes which have been revealed to the world in the conduct of those who minister in holy things, within a few years past, in all the different communions. In charity we must suppose that those who have exhibited such hardened guilt had no serious belief in the truth of the religion which it was their profession to teach.

But it may be said, and is often said, as a disparagement to Unitarianism, that in the places where it originated, and where it most prevails, there are weekly assemblies of persons who listen to men who were once Unitarian clergymen, but who now preach pure deism, who regard Jesus of Nazareth as a Jewish philosopher who was greatly in advance of his age, but whose doctrines have no other authority than that of being his opinions on matters of morals and religion.

This is triumphantly pointed out as conclusively showing the tendency of Unitarianism. This is just what the Orthodox have always predicted as the result of any departure from the old landmarks of the Trinitarian faith. How can you explain this fact, it is said, without admitting the deistic tendencies of Unitarianism ?

I answer, that we cannot have the benefits of consistent Protestantism, which is entire freedom of religious opinion and profession, without taking along with it its incidental evils. Where there is freedom of opinion, there will be occasional extravagance. And there is no other way of determining whether an opinion *is* extravagant or not, except by submitting it to the general judgment of mankind. That is the last resort, that is the final appeal. The *ex parte* judgment of existing Orthodoxy is not to be taken for the exponent of the decision of universal reason. We must have that decision, sooner or later, and the sooner we get it the sooner we shall have peace and rest. There is no way to get this verdict, except by entire freedom of opinion and profession.

I answer, in the second place, that religious opinions are now in a transition state all over the world. In times of revolution, there are always some who are disposed to carry things to extremes. Religious opinions, even in Protestant countries, have been matters of tradition and authority. Religious opinion is now passing over from passive tradition to individual conviction. In such a process, much, of course, must be discarded. It is not to be expected that every man will know precisely where to stop. Some, in repudiating what is false, will be in danger of rejecting what is true. In weeding out the tares, some of the wheat may chance to be rooted up.

But every position must be tried, in order to find out what is tenable. The investigation of truth is often like an algebraic process. A false quantity must be assumed, in order to discover the true one. Even if it could be shown that Unitarianism leads the mind, in some cases, to infidelity, there is no danger that it will stay there, unless infidelity be true. If infidelity be false, and Unitarianism be true, the mind will come back to Unitarianism. If Unitarianism is not infidelity, it will be shown that it is not. And the transition of a few bold speculators into infidelity will not destroy Unitarianism or Christianity, but only define Unitarianism on the side next to unbelief. The discussions of the last thirty years have defined Unitarianism on the side next to Orthodoxy. The shading off of a few cloudy thinkers into unbelief will lead to the discovery of the line where Christianity ends and infidelity begins. Books will be written, which will clearly show what is essential to Christianity and what is not. New treatises on the evidences will be composed, bringing out arguments on points which are now assailed for the first time, and adapted to the present phases of unbelief. When this is done, Christianity will stand stronger than ever.

In conclusion, I say that we have nothing to do with tendencies, but only with truth. It is presumptuous in us to stop to inquire whether truth will have a bad or good tendency. *All* truth must have a good tendency, or the world is based on falsehood. The only evil effect which truth can occasion in the world is temporary, and will be caused by the jar and disturbance that are produced in displacing error. In that sense Christianity itself came, not to introduce peace, but a sword.

The administration of Christianity itself has always been partly polemical. It has always consisted in the maintenance of truth, as well as the inculcation of goodness. The writings of the Apostles are, in no small degree, controversial. As long as man is fallible, he will always be liable to wander away from the truth, even after it has been discovered. Every age has its errors, which those who are set for the defence of the Gospel are obliged to combat. There is no discharge in that war, and it will never cease, to the end of time. If Unitarianism is Christianity, it will be shown to be so, and the Christian Church will become Unitarian. If it is not, it will be proved not to be, and Unitarianism will be abandoned. But the Christian Church will survive, for "it is founded on a rock, and the gates of hell shall not prevail against it."

An organized opposition, it is said, is no disadvantage to any cause. It keeps it healthy and strong. It arms it with the best arguments, and compels it to lop off all doctrines which are indefensible. Christianity itself is, perhaps, not exempted from this law. It is not improbable that it was the power which the Church early acquired, of putting down and silencing all opposition and dissent, which caused its doctrines to become so corrupted, and its usages so immoral. An organized deism may perhaps do Christianity good. If it have the power to set up an opposition to Christianity on its own ground, it may be no argument that Christianity is not true, but only that it is not properly administered. It is encumbered, perhaps, with errors which the age will not bear, and which it is necessary to prune away. It may be too limited in the range of its topics, or too technical and formal in the mode of their treatment. Its intellectual and literary culture may be behind the age. Deism can obtain a partial and a temporary success, only by cultivating those excellences which Christianity has neglected. Deism, then, may be made the instrument of driving the Christian Church into purity of doctrine and wisdom of administration. That it is weak in itself cannot be better shown than by its professing to be Christianity, adopting its forms, and imitating its great institutions, by which the world has been enlightened, refined, and sanctified.

DISCOURSE VII.

DOCTOR WATTS A UNITARIAN.

YE DO ERR, NOT KNOWING THE SCRIPTURES. — Matthew xxii. 29.

IT is the object of this discourse, according to the announcement of last Sunday evening, to lay before you the evidence which has convinced my own mind that Doctor Watts, the author of a poetical version of the Psalms of David and a great number of hymns for public worship, which have been so widely used, and done so much to uphold and perpetuate the doctrine of the Trinity, was led by the study of the Scriptures to renounce that doctrine, and died a Unitarian. I do not pretend to form your conclusions on this subject, but only candidly state to you the reasons of my own.

I do not, therefore, say that Unitarianism is true, and Trinitarianism false. Truth cannot be decided by counting suffrages, or appealing to distinguished names. I bring it forward as a curious and impressive fact, that one who had done so much to propagate the Trinitarian faith should have died a Unitarian at last. I advert to his conversion as the natural process of an inquiring, honest mind, when it comes to examine the Scriptural evidence of the doctrine of the Trinity, and those intrinsic and essential difficulties which it encounters when investigated in its own pure and abstract elements. I wish to call your attention to the evident reluctance with which he gave up his old ideas, and embraced the very views, or others still more Unitarian, which he so pathetically laments as having been embraced and promulgated by the great John Locke, who was his contemporary for a part of his life.

Doctor Watts was born in Southampton, England, 17 July, 1674. His father was a respectable citizen of that place, belonging to a congregation of Dissenters. He had a religious education, and early discovered a literary turn, which was gratified by opportunities for classical culture, and finally by a theological education at a divinity school in London, maintained by the Dissenters. His progress here was rapid, and at the age of twenty-four he became the clergyman of a congregation in Mark Lane, which afterwards built a chapel in Berry Street. The chapel, which, it is said, no one would take to be a church, is now exhibited as one of the curiosities of London.

He had early exhibited poetic genius, and it soon found exercise in the composition of hymns for public worship. For this species of composition, his talents were especially adapted. His warm piety and lively imagination gave him ready access to all who cherished devotional sentiments, and this number is always greater than that of those who lead a consistent Christian life.

Watts was educated a Calvinist of the strongest stamp, and a Trinitarian. These sentiments are woven into all his psalms and hymns. David is made a Trinitarian, though this doctrine was not broached till thirteen hundred years after his death, and he is made to discourse Calvinism in almost every page. But Doctor Watts felt himself justified in putting Trinitarianism into the Psalms on his own account. He did what was still more objectionable, though perfectly conscientiously at the time. The last three Psalms are mere doxologies, forms of praise to God which were long used for that purpose by the Jews. But it is to *one* God, and there is in them no hint of any plurality of persons in the Deity. He versified them, but added what he calls the Christian doxology, with this note: — "Since the Christian doxology is more used in Christian churches, I have added that also."

"To God the Father, God the Son,
And God the Spirit, three in one," &c.

This he varied in all the different metres, that it might be fitted on to all the Psalms of David, who lived and died as profoundly ignorant of the doctrine of the Trinity as he was of the continent of America. And what was the Christian doxology? Any thing found in the New Testament? By no means. It was this, — "Glory to the Father, and to the Son, and to the Holy Ghost," — and was a sectarian doxology framed by the Athanasians to drive the Arians out of the churches. And from Watts's day to this, the Psalms of David have been sung in the churches with this unauthorized and unscriptural appendage. His versification of this sectarian doxology, repeated from Sabbath to Sabbath, as if of Divine authority, has done more to perpetuate the belief in the doctrine of the Trinity than all the books of controversial divinity that were ever written. There is no sentiment whatever that might not thus be inculcated and perpetuated. What Doctor Watts afterwards thought of the Scriptural authority for these things, we shall see in the course of this examination.

He published his Hymns in the year 1707, at the age of thirty-three. His version of the Psalms was published twelve years later, in 1719. His first publication on the subject of the Trinity bears the date 1722, three years after the publication of his version of the Psalms.

In his Hymns, the doctrine of the Trinity is stated in the most obnoxious form: —

"This infant is the mighty God,
Come to be suckled and adored,
The Eternal Father, Prince of Peace,
The Son of David, and his Lord."

"Here at the cross, my dying God,
I lay my soul beneath thy love."

"Now by the bowels of my God,
His sharp distress, his sore complaints,
By his last groans, his dying blood,
I charge my soul to love the saints."

Here the birth, the suckling, and death of God are spoken of as fixed, familiar, and common ideas.

I have said that Doctor Watts began to publish his investigations into the doctrine of the Trinity in the year 1722. This date is important, as it fixes the period of his studies upon this subject, in which his opinions were formed and developed, to have been between the fortieth and fiftieth years of his age, in the very meridian of life. I am careful to make this statement, because it is said by those who wish to take from the authority of Watts's suffrage to Unitarian opinions, that he adopted them at a late period of life, after his mind had become enfeebled by age and sickness. I here read the testimony of his personal friend, Dr. Gibbons, that no such obscuration of his faculties ever took place.

"How it came to pass I know not, but that it has so happened is certain, that reports have been raised, propagated, and currently believed concerning the Doctor, that he has imagined such things concerning himself as would prove, if they were true, that he lost possession of himself, or suffered a momentary eclipse of his intellectual faculties; and I could refer my reader to a biographer who gives the world a grave narrative of the particulars of these wild reveries. But I take upon me, and feel myself happy to aver, that these reports were utterly and absolutely false and groundless; and I do this from my own knowledge and observation of him for several years, and some of them the years of his decay, when he was at the weakest; from the express declaration of Mr. Joseph Parker, his amanuensis for above twenty years, and who was in a manner ever with him; and, above all, from that of Mrs. Elizabeth Abney, the surviving daughter of Sir Thomas and Lady Abney, who lived in the same family with him all the time of the Doctor's residence there, a period of no less than thirty-six years. Can any evidence be more convincing and decisive?"

His investigations into the Scriptures and the ancient Hebrew writings led him gradually to abandon the personality of the Holy Ghost, and to conclude that the places in the New Testament in which it is mentioned as a person are *personifications*, and not descriptions of a real person. To the same conclusion he came as to the personality of the Word, which he thought to be a *power* of God. Thus, in his mind, God became one, by the gradual evanescence of what in his education he had learned to consider as the second and third persons of the Trinity. Hence it was that the Trinitarians complained that he reduced the Trinity to a trinity of names.

"Thus it appears," says Doctor Watts, in one of his treatises, "that as outward speech and breath are powers of the human body, as reason and vital activity or efficience are powers of the human soul, so the great God, in Scripture, has revealed himself to us as a glorious being, who has two eternal, essential, divine powers, which, in condescension to our weakness, he is pleased to describe by way of analogy to our souls and bodies; and this he doth by the terms *deber* and *ruach* in Hebrew, *logos* and *pneuma* in Greek, and in English, *word* and *spirit*, or *speech* and *breath*, or *reason* and *vital activity* or *efficience*."

"Thus I have represented the clearest and best ideas I have yet attained concerning the Spirit of God, who is generally called the third person in the sacred Trinity. As Christ, in his divine nature, is represented as the eternal word or wisdom of the Father, which perhaps may include in it the power of knowledge, or knowledge and volition; so the Spirit seems to be another divine power, which may be called the power of efficience. And though it is sometimes described in Scripture as a personal agent, after the manner of Jewish and Eastern writers, yet if we put all the Scriptures relating to this subject together, and view them in a correspondent light, the Spirit of God does not seem to be described as a distinct spirit from the Father, or as another conscious mind, but as an eternal, essential power, belonging to the Father, whereby all things are effected ; and thus the supreme godhead of the blessed Spirit is maintained in its glory."

This, you perceive, is pure Sabellianism, or Unitarianism in its simplest form. The Unitarian believes in the godhead of the Spirit in this sense, — that it is God himself, just as the spirit of man is man himself. This accords precisely with the comparison of Paul : — " For what man knoweth the things of a man, save the spirit of man which is in him ? Even so the things of God knoweth no man, but the Spirit of God."

But having arrived at the conclusion, that the Holy Ghost is " an eternal, essential power belonging to the Father," it was natural that so conscientious a man as Doctor Watts, who had composed so many doxologies to the Holy Ghost, should feel some anxiety as to the propriety of making the Holy Ghost a distinct object of worship. In the course of his inquiry, he states his conclusion in the form of an *objection* to the practice of ascribing divine honors to the Holy Ghost. He then answers the objection.

" Objection. If the Spirit of God be properly a power of the Divine nature, or a distinct principle of action, and not a real and proper person, or distinct intelligent being, how can we offer a doxology to the Spirit, and ascribe honor and glory to him, together with the Father and the Son ?

" Answer I. Though I think it may be very proper, upon some occasions, to join the Holy Spirit in a doxology, and to offer glory and praise to him, together with the Father and the Son, yet I think it may be affirmed, that there is not any one plain and express instance in all the Scripture of a doxology directly and distinctly addressed to the Holy Spirit Perhaps one reason, among others, may be, because both the Father and the Son, considered as God-man, are proper distinct persons, while the proper, distinct, and real character of the Spirit is that of a divine power or principle of action, and it is only personalized by idioms of speech.

"Now, though there may be two or three examples of such a doxology in the writers of the first three centuries, and though it may be properly practised in many cases, yet if there be neither precept nor pattern for it in Scripture, it ought not to be esteemed so constant and so necessary a part of worship as modern ages have made it, and as I once thought it to be."

"Answer II. Since I believe the Spirit of God to be coeternal with God, and essential and necessary to his very being, and in that sense true God, and since he is represented in Scripture in a personal manner, or under the character of a distinct person, therefore forms of praise may be lawfully addressed to him, as well as peculiar blessings may be said to descend from him. Though the Scripture has not taught us distinctly to offer praise and honor to the Holy Spirit, yet it has taught us to hearken to the voice of the Spirit, to obey the Spirit, to hope and wait for the enlightening, the sanctifying, and the comforting influences of the Spirit, and not to resist him ; and since the Holy Spirit is true God, I think it follows, by evident consequence, that we may offer him the sacrifice of praise for the blessings which he bestows. There is no more necessity that he should be a real, proper, distinct person, or another conscious mind, in order to receive such addresses, than in order to bestow such blessings. A figurative personality is sufficient for both.

" Answer III. I add yet further, that if the Holy Spirit had never been represented in a personal manner in Scripture, yet a distinct power of the Divine nature may surely be as proper an object of doxology as a divine attribute or perfection, which does not seem to carry in the idea of it so great a distinction as a divine power. I think there is no impropriety in ascribing praise and glory to the wisdom or the grace of God. May we not properly use such language as this : — ' We give thanks to the grace of God ' ; ' Let us give praise to the almighty power of God ' ; ' Glory be given to God and his mercy ' ; ' Let God the Father, and his eternal wisdom, and his love, be glorified for ever ' ? Now, if these expressions may be sometimes used on particular occasions with propriety and devotion, though we are not necessarily bound to use them, I see no reason why we may not, upon particular occasions, ascribe glory to God the Father, to his eter-

nal Word, and his almighty Spirit, even though the Word, together with the Spirit, considered purely in their divine nature, may be really distinct principles of action in the godhead, and not real, proper, distinct beings.

"It may be still further argued: Suppose the powers, or even the attributes or agencies of God, were expressed in yet more metaphorical language, yet they might lawfully be doxologized. May we not say, 'Glory be to God and his victorious arm'; or 'to his watchful eye'? Or, may we not ascribe 'glory to the Father and the Son, and their counsels of mercy,' and such like? Surely, then, the blessed Spirit, whatsoever be his philosophical character or idea in the godhead, may receive ascriptions of glory with as much propriety.

"But if all these considerations were not sufficient to make us allow of doxologies to the Holy Spirit, I say, in the last place,

"Answer IV. As in some Scriptures the Spirit of God seems to include in it the whole idea of godhead, acting by the blessed Spirit, why may we not ascribe glory to the blessed Spirit under this idea? May we not say, 'Glory be given to God, who sanctifies and comforts us by his blessed Spirit,' as well as 'Glory to him who sustains the supreme dignity of godhead under the idea of a father'? Perhaps, if this sense be put upon the words, it may please some persons better, who are sincere and zeal-

ous believers of the doctrine of the Trinity, according to the common orthodox explication; for this idea of the Spirit approaches nearer to the orthodox scheme, wherein the whole divine essence is included in each person, together with a distinct modality of that essence which is called the personality. Upon any of these principles which I have mentioned, there is sufficient ground for a doxology to be given to the blessed Spirit, without supposing him to be a distinct intelligent being, or another mind."

One of the greatest difficulties in the way of the doctrine of the Trinity, to a person who conceives of God as one pure Spirit, has been the idea of *derivation* contained in it. The Athanasian creed, which is a scholastic statement of the Trinity, asserts that the Son is *begotten* of the Father, and the Holy Ghost *proceeds* from the Father and the Son. Doctor Watts perceived the difficulty of reconciling his theory of the Word and Spirit being "two eternal, essential powers belonging to the Father," with the common hypothesis of derivation. He notices the incongruity, not to retract his own conclusion, but to call in question the hypothesis of derivation itself, as something, if not unintelligible, at least too incomprehensible for his understanding. The turning point of the proof that Doctor Watts was a Unitarian is his admission that the Holy Spirit is not a person, but a *personification* of an "eternal, essential power belonging to the Father." It is no wonder, then, that his understanding rebelled against the derivation of a mere personification.

"Objection. If the Spirit of God be properly a power, or principle of agency in the Divine nature, how can it be said, according to the common doctrine of divines, that he proceeds from the Father and the Son?

"Answer I. It was proper, in the objection, to name the common doctrine of divines, and not the doctrine of Scripture, for the text from which this is derived, John fifteenth, twenty-sixth, only saith that the Spirit cometh forth, or proceedeth from the Father, and that he is sent by the Son. But the Scripture never says that the Spirit, as to his nature, proceeds from the Son; no, nor properly from the Father, as to his nature, though his mission is originally from the Father; and perhaps it is in this sense that he is described in Scripture as proceeding from the Father, because he is the divine, efficient power of the Father, which is employed in all divine operations.

"The notion of the Spirit's procession, or derivation, as to his essence and personality, both from the Father and the Son, how current so ever it has been, is not a plain and express Scriptural doctrine, but a human inference drawn from this doubtful argument, viz.: — 'That if the Spirit be sent by the Son as to his commission in the economy, he must proceed from the Son as to his nature, existence, or personality.' But this argument, if thoroughly examined, has no great force in it. The Greek churches were not influenced by it; for in elder and later days they have supposed the Spirit to proceed from the Father only, though they confess he is sent by the Son, as well as by the Father; and this seems to come nearer to the plain and express language of Scripture.

"The common explication of the eternal generation of the Son, and eternal procession of the Spirit from the Father and Son, which was authorized in the Latin churches, was derived down to us from the Popish schoolmen; though it is now become a part of the established, or orthodox faith, in most of the Protestant nations, because at the Reformation they knew no better way to explain the doctrine of the sacred Trinity. They contented themselves to say it was incomprehensible, and thus forbid all further inquiries. But this scholastic, Popish explication of the manner of the derivation of the Son and Spirit from the Father is, perhaps, the most inconceivable and indefensible part of all the common scheme of the Trinity which is called orthodox. I heartily agree to several other parts of it, viz.: — 'That God is one infinite and eternal spirit, or conscious being. That the Divine essence is but one and the same, though distinguished into three sacred persons.' But their account of the generation and the procession, that is, of the manner of the derivation of the Word and Spirit from the Father, seems to me, at present, to be a set of words, of which I can attain no ideas, invented by subtle and metaphysical schoolmen, to guard and fence, as far as possible, against the charge of inconsistency, and was never designed to convey a clear conception to the mind of Christians. Let us take a short survey of what this scholastic notion is.

"The most approved writers represent it thus: — 'That the generation of the Son is the Father's communication of his own selfsame, individual, self-existent essence to the Son, together with the personal property of being begotten, in and by which property he differs from the Father.' And, 'That the procession of the Spirit is a communication of the selfsame individual, self-existent essence, both from the Father and the Son, unto the Spirit, together with the personal property of spiration, or proceeding, by which property he differs from the Father and the Son.'

"How strange so ever this language appears to persons who seek for ideas together with words, I seriously profess this is the justest, truest, and, I think, the plainest description that I can give of this opinion. If it be possible to make it plainer, I will repeat the same in another form of words.

"The scholastic scheme supposes the eternal generation of the Son to be a sort of repetition of the selfsame numerical Divine essence of the Father, together with some new personal property, called filiation, which joined to the Divine essence makes up the person of the Son. And that this repetition or reproduction of the same Divine essence with its new personality is owing to the Father only.

"It also supposes the procession of the Holy Spirit to be another sort of repetition of the self-same numerical Divine essence of the Father, together with some new personal property, called procession, which, joined to the Divine essence, makes up the person of the Holy Spirit. And that this repetition or reproduction of the same Divine essence with its new personality is owing to the Father and the Son conjointly; or, as some rather say, it is from the Father as the original principle, by the Son as a medium.

"There have been some witers, indeed, who thought it was not proper to say of the Divine essence itself that it did generate, or could be generated or derived; and therefore they supposed only the personality of the Son to be generated, or derived from the Father, and the personality of the Spirit to proceed or be derived from the Father and the Son. But when you inquire what these personalities are, they can only tell you that it is filiation, or sonship, and spiration, or procession. Upon the whole, therefore, according to this opinion, it is sonship is generated, and procession proceeds. But the generality of the scholastic or orthodox Trinitarians go into the former sentiments, of the generation and procession of the Divine essence itself, together with the distinct personalities.

"With a solemn and unfeigned veneration I reverence the names and memories of those excellent men, those learned and pious authors of the last age, who asserted and defended these opinions. Nor do I think the devotion, and zeal, and piety, of our present times equal to theirs. But when I inquire of my own heart, whether ever I could form any ideas of all this sort of language, while I was taught it in my younger days, and firmly assented to these sounds, I must honestly confess I could not. Sometimes I was ready to inquire further; but then I satisfied all my inquisitive thoughts with this general notion, that it was incomprehensible. I found it sufficiently evident in Scripture, that the Father was God, that the Son was God, and the Holy Spirit was God; and that they were usually represented in Scripture as three persons. And though I had no distinct idea of the *modus* of it, yet I thought myself sufficiently defended and intrenched in the forms of scholastic language, and armed with that set of phrases which make up this part of the common or orthodox explication, without being too solicitous about conceiving that which was asserted to be utterly inconceivable."

I am persuaded that no fair-minded person, after reading this, can ever again believe that the writer of it was a Trinitarian, as that word is generally understood. And yet, while he himself had substantially renounced the Trinity, still his Psalms and Hymns, the copy-right of which he had sold, were not converting, but educating, by the mere force of authority and repetition, thousands and thousands into the very belief which he had given up as not countenanced by Scripture or reason. The Christian world went on worshipping the Holy Ghost as a person, in the use of the Hymns of Doctor Watts, when he himself had become convinced that it was a mere personification.

The contemporaries of a man are the best judges of the significance and tendency of his writings. His biographer subjoins the following note to his writings on the Trinity : — "Those, who wish to see what some of Doctor Watts's pious and learned contemporaries thought of his Trinitarian writings, may peruse Dr. Abraham Taylor's 'Scripture Doctrine of the Trinity vindicated, in Opposition to Mr. Watts's Scheme of One Divine Person and Two Divine Powers.' Mr. Hurrion, also, a very able writer, published a set of discourses, entitled, 'The Scripture Doctrine of the Proper Divinity, Real Personality, &c., of the Holy Spirit, stated and defended.'"

With regard to the second person of the Trinity, Doctor Watts's inquiries led him to abandon the common hypothesis as to the distinct subsistence and personality of what is usually termed the divine nature of Christ. The only divine nature which he considered the Scriptures to teach as existing in Christ was the in-dwelling of the whole Deity.

His sentiments on this subject are brought out in a distinct treatise, which he published under the following title : — "Useful and Important Questions concerning Jesus the Son of God." In that treatise he first institutes the inquiry, whether the expression "Son," and "Son of God," applied to Christ, were intended to assert any participation in the essence of God. This he conclusively proves in the negative. He enumerates five different senses in which the title "Son of God" has been alleged to be applied to Christ. The first of them, which is that of participation in Deity, he emphatically rejects.

"The first of these senses is patronized by many writers, viz. : — 'That an eternal, inconceivable generation of the person of the Son, by the person of the Father, in the sameness of the Divine essence, consubstantial, coequal, and coeternal with the Father, is included in the name Son of God.'

"But I am persuaded that this can never be the sense of this name in those several texts before cited ; they can never signify that it is necessary to salvation to believe Christ to be the 'eternal Son of God,' as a distinct person in the same Divine essence, proceeding from the Father by such an eternal and incomprehensible generation. For,

"I. If this be ever so true, yet it is confessed to be inconceivable. Now, if it be so very inconceivable, so mysterious and sublime a doctrine, then I do not think the gracious God would put such a difficult test upon the faith of young disciples, poor, illiterate men and women, in the very beginning of the Gospel, and exclude them from heaven for not believing it.

"II. Nor, indeed, is this eternal generation and consubstantial sonship clearly enough revealed in Scripture for us to make it a fundamental article in any age, and to damn all who do not receive it. I cannot see evidence enough in the word of God to make the salvation of all mankind, the poor and the ignorant, the laboring men and the children, even in such a day of knowledge as this is, to depend on such a doctrine, which the most learned and pious Christians in all ages have confessed to be attended with so many difficulties, — which, after the labor and study of near fourteen hundred years, is so inconceivable in itself, and was at first so obscurely revealed ; much less can I suppose this notion of the Son of God could be made a necessary and fundamental article in those dawnings of the Gospel-day."

As a counterpart to the common doctrine of the Trinity, three persons in the Deity, it has been generally maintained that the distinction between them was of such a nature as to admit of personal intercourse. They could converse together and make mutual stipulations. In the theology which was current in the age of Doctor Watts, there were long conversations imagined to have taken place between God the Father and God the Son, in relation to the redemption of mankind.

With the views which he had adopted, all such representations could not seem less than absurd. In the course of his inquiry, he takes up the question whether there is any foundation for such representations. He comes to the conclusion, that there is none whatever.

"The common or scholastic explication of the Trinity, which has been long universally received by our Protestant writers, and has been called orthodox for these several hundred years, is this, viz.:—That God is but one simple, infinite, and eternal Spirit. Hence it follows, that the Divine essence, powers, and essential properties of the Father, the Son, and the Spirit, in the godhead, are numerically the very same essence, powers, and essential properties; that it is the same numerical consciousness, understanding, will, and power, which belongs to the Father, that belongs also to the Son and to the Holy Spirit; and that the sacred Three are distinguished only by the superadded, relative properties of paternity, filiation, and procession; but their thoughts, ideas, volitions, and agencies, according to this hypothesis, must be the very same numerical thoughts, ideas, actions, and volitions, in all the sacred Three."

He then goes on to quote from a sermon by Flavel, a popular sermonizer of those times, in which he details the stipulations of a covenant made between the Father and the Son, before the foundation of the world. "Consider," says Flavel, "the persons transacting and dealing with each other in this covenant. These are God the Father, and God the Son, the former as a creditor, the latter as a surety. The Father stands upon satisfaction, the Son engages to give it," &c.

"Now, in reading over such accounts," says Doctor Watts, "of stipulation and contract between the Father and the Son, before the foundation of the world, what proper conceptions can we frame, or what clear ideas can we possibly have, while we suppose nothing but Christ's divine nature transacting this affair with the Father; and while, at the same time, we believe the Divine essence, perfections, and powers, the understanding, will, thought, and consciousness, of the Father and of the Son to be numerically one and the same, since in the godhead, or Divine nature, they are but one and the same infinite Spirit? The mere personalities, viz. paternity and filiation, cannot consult and transact these affairs in a way of contract, proposal, and consent. It is nothing but two distinct consciousnesses and two distinct wills can enter into such a covenant; but in the common explication of the Trinity, the distinct personalities of the Father and the Son do not make any real distinct consciousnesses or distinct wills in the one infinite Spirit.

"And let it be further noted, also, that, according to several of the articles of this covenant, one of these beings or persons covenanting seems to be inferior to the other, and to be capable of receiving orders, commission, support, and recompense from the other. But if only the deity of Christ existed at that time, and the deity of Christ and of the Father have but one and the same numerical consciousness and volition, one and the same numerical power and glory, what need of orders and commissions, what need of promises of support and recompense? How can the pure godhead of Christ be supported or be recompensed by the Father, who has eternally the same numerical glory and power?

"In short, all these sacred and pathetic representations of stipulation and articles, in the common scheme, can amount to no more, in our clear ideas, and in a proper conception of things, than the simple decree or volition of the one eternal, infinite Spirit.

"I grant we may suppose the great God, in a figurative manner of speech, consulting thus with his own wisdom, with the divine powers or principles of agency in his own nature, as a man may be figuratively said to consult with his own understanding, or reason, or conscience. But, in literal and proper language, it seems to be nothing else but an absolute decree of the great God, that the man Christ Jesus, when formed and united to godhead, should undertake and fulfil this work, four thousand years after this world was made. And thus, according to the common hypothesis, that very intelligent being which was to come into flesh, and to sustain all the real sufferings, gave no such early antecedent consent to this covenant. It was only the godhead of Christ, which is impassible and could really suffer nothing, did decree that the human nature should exist hereafter, that it should be united to the godhead, and should sustain agoniės and death for the sins of men.

"I would inquire further, also, according to this explication of things, what possible difference can we conceive between the love of the Father in sending his Son, and the love of the Son in consenting to be sent on this compassionate errand, if there were not two distinct consciousnesses and two distinct wills, if it was only one simple, numerical volition of the great God? And how doth this abate our grand ideas of the distinct and condescending love of our blessed Saviour, in his consent to this covenant, since that part of him which really suffered, that is, his inferior nature, had then no existence, and therefore could give no consent to this early covenant of redemption?"

At the time when Doctor Watts lived, Biblical criticism had scarcely begun to be cultivated, and, according to the principles of interpretation then received, he considered himself obliged to understand in their literal sense those passages in which Christ speaks of himself as "having come down from heaven," as "having been in heaven," &c. To account for these passages, he considered the human soul of Christ to have preëxisted, and to have come into the world. The common supposition, that the divine nature of Christ left heaven and came on earth, he treats as an utter impossibility, wholly inconsistent with the very nature of Deity.

"For the divine nature of Christ, how distinct so ever it is supposed to be from God the Father, yet can never leave the Father's bosom, can never divest itself of any one joy or felicity that it was ever possessed of, nor lose even the least degree of it; nor could God the Father ever dismiss the divine nature of his Son from his own bosom. Godhead must have eternal and complete beatitude, joy, and glory, and can never be dispossessed of it. Godhead can sustain no real sorrow, suffering, or pain. The utmost that can be said concerning the deity of Christ is, that there is a relative imputation of the sorrows, sufferings, and pains of the human nature to the divine, because of the union between them; so that the sufferings acquire a sort of divine dignity and merit hereby. It is granted, indeed, that this relative and imputative suffering may be sufficient in a legal sense to advance the dignity of the sacrifice of Christ to a complete and equivalent satisfaction for sin; yet the exceeding greatness of the love of the Father and the Son does not seem to be so sensibly manifested to us hereby, for all this abasement of the godhead of Christ is merely relative, and not real.

"And as it is plain that the divine nature of Christ could not be separated from the bosom of the Father when he came into this world and took flesh upon him, so neither could the human nature leave the bosom of the Father, if it had no prior existence and was never there. Therefore, in the common scheme, all this glorious and pathetic representation of the love of Christ, in leaving the joys and glories of heaven, when he came to dwell upon earth, has no ideas belonging to it, and it can be true in no sense, since it can neither be attributed to the human nor to the divine nature of Christ, nor to his whole person. I grant, that, by the figure of communication of properties, what is true of one nature may be attributed to the whole person, or sometimes to the other nature ; yet that which is not true concerning either nature of Christ separated, nor concerning the two natures united, cannot be attributed to him at all. So that 'parting with the bosom of his Father,' and 'forsaking the joys and glories he possessed there,' are, according to the common scheme, words of which we have no ideas."

The only remaining part of the discussion, from which I have space to quote, is that in which he clearly proves that Christ had no such divine nature as is usually conceived of as the second person of the Trinity. The only divine nature which he had was the indwelling of the whole Deity in him. He enters upon the inquiry by the formal statement of the question, — " Is the godhead of Christ and the godhead of the Father one and the same godhead ? "

" If the divine nature of Christ be another distinct principle of self-consciousness and volition, another distinct spiritual being, or another spirit, this approaches so near to the doctrine of another God, that it is very hard to distinguish it. For, so far as our ideas of arithmetic and reason can reach, this seems to be a plain truth : — ' If one infinite spirit be one God, two or three infinite spirits must be two or three gods.' And though the patrons of this opinion suppose these three spirits to be so nearly united as to be called one God, merely to avoid the charge of polytheism, yet it must be granted that this one God must, then, be one complex infinite being, or spirit, made up of three single infinite beings or spirits ; which is such a notion of the one true God as I think reason nor revelation will admit. And yet, if this were the true notion of the one God, it is very strange that Scripture should not clearly and expressly reveal it.

" When Christ expresses his own godhead in the New Testament, it is by declaring his oneness with the Father, that is, the union of the man Christ Jesus with the same godhead that is in the Father. ' I and the Father are one.' — John tenth, thirtieth. 'He that hath seen me hath seen the Father ; I am in the Father, and the Father in me ; the Father that dwelleth in me, he doeth the works.' — John fourteenth, ninth, tenth. And it must be observed, that there is not any place in the New Testament where the miraculous works of Christ are ascribed to any distinct godhead of his own, different from the godhead of the Father, or the godhead of the Spirit of God that dwelt in him. And it is not reasonable to suppose that Christ would have always used these modes of speaking, and attributed his own works to the Father and his Spirit, if he himself had another godhead or divine nature different from that of the Father and the Spirit. For why should his miraculous works be attributed to the aid of another infinite spirit, which was not united to the man Jesus, and never be ascribed at all to that distinct spirit which is supposed to be united to him ? I am sure this sort of representation leads our thoughts away from supposing Christ to have any godhead at all, if it be not the same as the Father's.

"If the godhead of Christ be another distinct spiritual being, different from the godhead of the Father, I do not see any fair and reasonable manner how the Trinitarian can solve the difficulties which arise from those Scriptures where God the Father is represented as the *only true God*, and under that idea distinguished from Jesus Christ ; as John seventeenth, third, — 'To know thee, the only true God, and Jesus Christ whom thou hast sent.' First Corinthians eighth, sixth, — 'To us there is but one God, the Father, of whom are all things, ... and one Lord, Jesus Christ, by whom are all things.' Ephesians fourth, fifth, sixth, — 'There is one Lord, one faith, one baptism, one God and Father of all.' Now, we can scarce suppose the highest nature of Jesus Christ to be another infinite spirit, distinct from God the Father, without excluding it from godhead by these express Scriptures; but they may easily be explained to admit Christ's godhead, if we suppose Christ to be spoken of in these places chiefly in his inferior characters as man and mediator; and yet he may be united to, and inhabited by, the one true and eternal God, who is at other times called the Father, as being vested with different relative properties, and first in the great economy, as I have sufficiently shown in other papers."

If any one, after reading these extracts, can continue to count Doctor Watts a Trinitarian, let him read his solemn "Address to the Deity," which was prefixed to one of the last pamphlets he ever published. In it you will perceive the breathings of the same devotion which pervades his Psalms and Hymns, together with a reluctance to abandon his old theological opinions, with which his devotional feelings had become early associated. In one part of it, there is a striking acknowledgment that the doctrine of the Trinity had nearly driven him into infidelity.

There seems to be something almost providential in the manner in which this prayer has been preserved, as evidence of the last thoughts of Doctor Watts. It was prefixed to a treatise on the Trinity, containing a summary of all he had ever written upon the subject. Fifty copies of it only were published. His Orthodox friends, taking the alarm lest it should destroy his popularity and injure his influence, persuaded him to recall the edition and commit it to the flames. One copy only remained, and was afterwards found in a bookseller's shop at Southampton, in the year 1796, just half a century from its publication. The tract was entitled, "A Faithful Inquiry after the Ancient and Original Doctrine of the Trinity taught by Christ and his Apostles."

Doctor Lardner, one of the most honest of men, who had the best means of knowing his sentiments, as his nephew was one of his executors, saw him often during the last years of his life, and had the examination of his papers after his death, testifies, — "The last thoughts of Doctor Watts were completely Unitarian."

"Dear and blessed God! hadst thou been pleased, in any one plain Scripture, to have informed me which of the different opinions about the Holy Trinity, among the contending parties of Christians, had been true, thou knowest with how much zeal, satisfaction, and joy my unbiased heart would have opened itself to receive and embrace the divine discovery. Hadst thou told me plainly, in any single text, that the Father, Son, and Holy Spirit are three real distinct persons in thy Divine nature, I had never suffered myself to be bewildered in so many doubts, nor embarrassed with so many strong fears of assenting to the mere inventions of men, instead of Divine doctrine; but I should have humbly and immediately accepted thy words, so far as it was possible for me to understand them, as the only rule of my faith. Or hadst thou been pleased so to express and include this proposition in the several scattered parts of thy book, from whence my reason and conscience might with ease find out and with certainty infer this doctrine, I should have joyfully employed all my reasoning powers, with their utmost skill and activity, to have found out this inference, and ingrafted it into my soul."

"Thou hast taught me, Holy Father, by thy prophets, that the way of holiness in the times of the Gospel, or under the kingdom of the Messiah, shall be a highway, a plain and easy path; so that the wayfaring man, or the stranger, 'though a fool, shall not err therein.' And thou hast called the poor and the ignorant, the mean and the foolish things of this world, to the knowledge of thyself and thy Son, and taught them to receive and partake of the salvation which thou hast provided. But how can such weak creatures ever take in so strange, so difficult, and so abstruse a doctrine as this, in the explication and defence whereof, multitudes of men, even men of learning and piety, have lost themselves in infinite subtilties of dispute, and endless mazes of darkness? And can this strange and perplexing notion of three real persons going to make up one true God be so necessary and so important a part of that Christian doctrine, which, in the Old Testament and the New, is represented as so plain and so easy, even to the meanest understandings?"

"Great God, who seest all things! thou hast beheld what busy temptations have been often fluttering about my heart, to call it off from these laborious and difficult inquiries, and to give up thy word and thy Gospel as an unintelligible book, and betake myself to the light of nature and reason; but thou hast been pleased by thy Divine power to scatter these temptations, and fix my heart and hope again upon that Saviour and that eternal life which thou hast revealed in thy word, and proposed therein to our knowledge and our acceptance. Blessed be the name of my God, that has not suffered me to abandon the Gospel of his Son Jesus! And blessed be that Holy Spirit that has kept me attentive to the truth delivered in thy Gospel, and inclined me to wait longer in my search of these Divine truths, under the hope of thy gracious illumination!"

Such were the last thoughts of a pious and learned

man, after more than twenty years of examination of the sacred Scriptures. His Psalms and Hymns were comparatively a juvenile work, written wholly, as he acknowledges, while he was under the influence of opinions which were entirely traditionary, and adopted by him without even comprehending the terms in which they were expressed.

While he was acknowledging that the Trinity amounted to nothing more than one God in one person and two divine powers, thousands and thousands were appending a Trinitarian doxology to the Psalms of David on his authority, — "To God the Father, God the Son, and God the Spirit, three in one," — when at the same time he himself had given up the personality of the Holy Ghost, and acknowledged that there was no Scriptural authority for addressing a doxology to it at all, any more than there is for addressing a doxology to God's arm or eye !

THE END.

www.ingramcontent.com/pod-product-compliance
Lightning Source LLC
LaVergne TN
LVHW011238110826
845150LV00006B/1672

* 9 7 8 1 4 2 5 5 1 3 8 3 2 *